# ADVANCE PRAISE FOR *BEYOND BLOOD*

"Beyond Blood courageously humanizes and reconnects us with the 25 million precious souls still suffering from HIV/AIDS in sub-Saharan Africa today. [This] is the powerful story of what happens when you say YES to Jesus. If you will want to think, feel, and love more like Jesus, read this book."

**SANTIAGO "JIMMY" MELLADO**
PRESIDENT & CEO, COMPASSION INTERNATIONAL

"Dr. Martin Luther King, Jr. said that—Life's most persistent and urgent question is, 'What are you doing for others?' Well, it's clear that in this book Cornel, Duncan, and Justin have answered this question through profound and strategic action. They've shown us all that through unity and sacrifice a nation can be transformed."

**SAM COLLIER**
INTERNATIONAL SPEAKER, NATIONAL TV & RADIO-PODCAST HOST

"At its heart, the Gospel is relational. *Beyond Blood* tells the story of relationships in both ordinary and extraordinary situations and reminds us all that redemption and hope grow best in the fertile ground of relationship."

**ANDY STANLEY**
AUTHOR, COMMUNICATOR & FOUNDER OF NORTH POINT MINISTRIES

"A reminder that all great leaders are ordinary people who simply said yes, and that we all have the capacity to change the world."

**JOHN C. MAXWELL**
AUTHOR, SPEAKER & COACH

"A remarkable example of how profound relationships among people who are called to serve can change lives forever."

**CHERYL BACHELDER**
AUTHOR OF *DARE TO SERVE: HOW TO DRIVE SUPERIOR RESULTS BY SERVING OTHERS*

"*Beyond Blood* takes us into places of raw reality seldom seen in glossy mission reports. In the midst of Africa's AIDS devastation, three unlikely young men find their calling to become powerful agents of hope and healing. The ministry that emerges is a model of holistic transformation. Instructive and inspiring!"

**ROBERT "BOB" LUPTON**
FOUNDER, FOCUSED COMMUNITY STRATEGIES (FCS), ATLANTA, GA; AUTHOR OF *TOXIC CHARITY, CHARITY DETOX* & *THEIRS IS THE KINGDOM*

"The power of diverse relationships is perfectly illustrated in this compelling story. It reminds the reader that no matter who or where they are, they have the opportunity to make an impact."

**RODNEY BULLARD**
EXECUTIVE DIRECTOR, CHICK-FIL-A FOUNDATION

"*Beyond Blood* is a compelling story of faith, hope, and love in the face of one of the world's most challenging crises. Cornel, Duncan, and Justin and the team at CARE for AIDS are an inspiration and an example for all of us to make a difference wherever we are and no matter our circumstances."

**TIM TASSOPOULOS**
PRESIDENT, CHICK-FIL-A, INC.

"In *Beyond Blood*, we see friendship and faith that leads to courageous action in addressing the AIDS pandemic. When other people ran away, Duncan, Justin, and Cornel ran towards those in need—serving with big hearts and open hands. I loved this book, and I know you will too!"

**PETER GREER**
PRESIDENT & CEO, HOPE INTERNATIONAL; CO-AUTHOR OF *MISSION DRIFT*

"*Beyond Blood* weaves together the inspiring stories of three men who grew up worlds apart, yet still became brothers. Together they created a culture of transformation for thousands of families. If you want your life to count for something big, you should read this book!"

**RANDY GRAVITT**
CEO OF INTEGREAT LEADERSHIP; CO-AUTHOR OF *UNSTUCK*

HOPE & HUMANITY
IN THE FORGOTTEN FIGHT
AGAINST AIDS

# BEYOND BLOOD

DUNCAN KIMANI KAMAU

JUSTIN T. MILLER

CORNEL ONYANGO NYAYWERA

GREENLEAF
BOOK GROUP PRESS

Published by Greenleaf Book Group Press
Austin, Texas
www.gbgpress.com

Distributed by Greenleaf Book Group

For ordering information or special discounts for bulk purchases, please contact Greenleaf Book Group at PO Box 91869, Austin, TX  78709, 512.891.6100.

Design and composition by Lindsay Miller
Cover design by Lindsay Miller

Publisher's Cataloging-in-Publication data is available.

Print ISBN: 978-1-62634-661-1

eBook ISBN: 978-1-62634-662-8

Part of the Tree Neutral® program, which offsets the number of trees consumed in the production and printing of this book by taking proactive steps, such as planting trees in direct proportion to the number of trees used: www.treeneutral.com

TreeNeutral

Printed in the United States of America on acid-free paper

19 20 21 22 23 24 25   11 10 9 8 7 6 5 4 3 2

First Edition

FOR KIM,

THIS STORY WOULD NOT EXIST

WITHOUT YOU. YOU SAW SOMETHING

IN ALL OF US THAT WE COULDN'T EVEN

SEE IN OURSELVES. YOUR LEGACY LIVES

ON IN US AND THE UNTOLD OTHERS YOU

IMPACTED. UNTIL WE MEET AGAIN, WE

WILL LOVE GENEROUSLY, ADVENTURE

BOLDLY, AND WALK FAITHFULLY WITH

GOD AS YOU TAUGHT US.

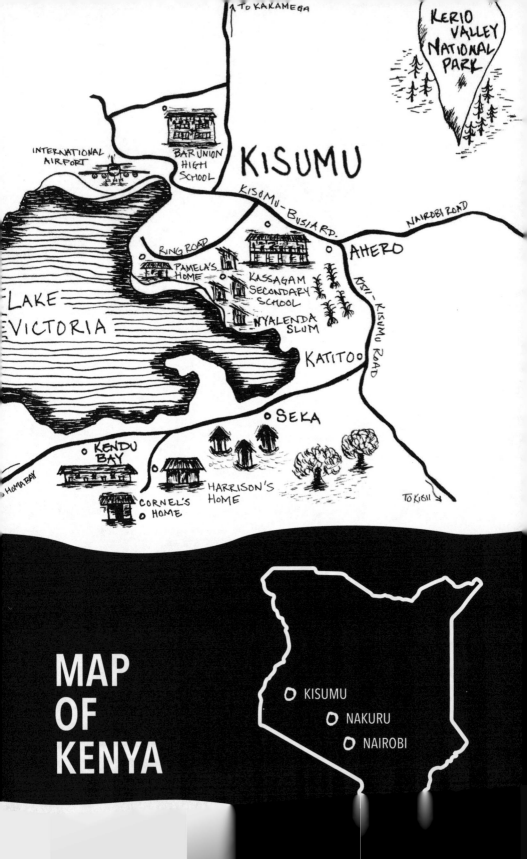

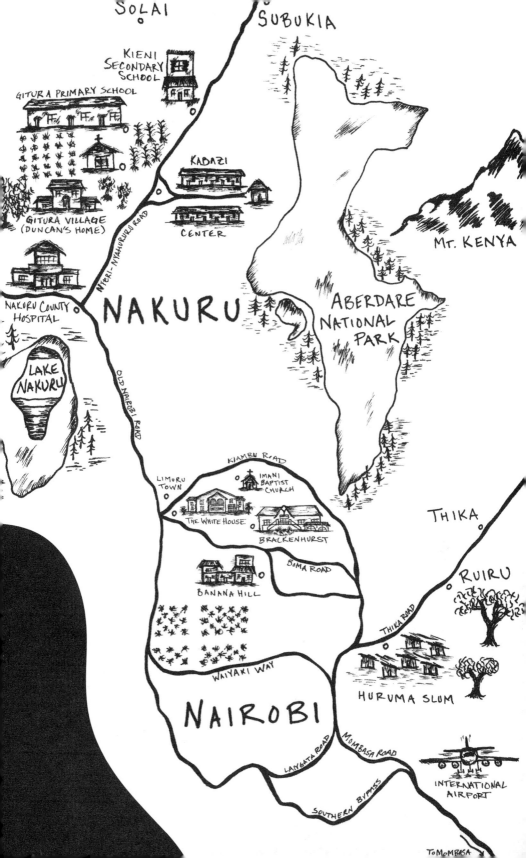

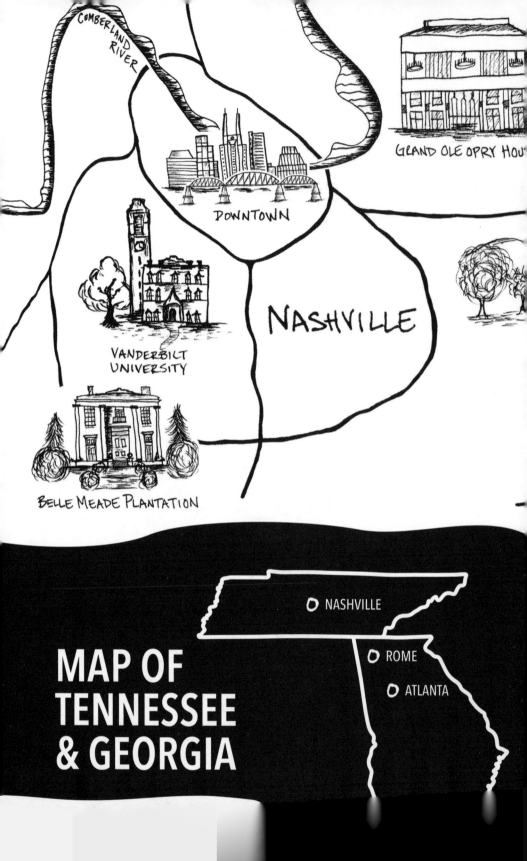

COMBERLAND RIVER

GRAND OLE OPRY HOU

DOWNTOWN

NASHVILLE

VANDERBILT UNIVERSITY

BELLE MEADE PLANTATION

# MAP OF TENNESSEE & GEORGIA

O NASHVILLE

O ROME

O ATLANTA

# INTRODUCTION

When our taxi dropped us off, I assumed we'd taken a wrong turn. It would have been an easy mistake, since there were no street signs to guide our way. We were dropped off at a rickety wooden bridge over black water that was only passable on foot. We crossed the bridge one by one, holding our breath, partially because of the smell and partially because of the fear of falling. After the bridge was a swamp, stagnant and brown from the recent rainy season. We rolled up our jeans and trudged through the water, toward the lone house that stood on the horizon. I wasn't surprised by how dilapidated the house was. I wasn't caught off guard by the heavy stench of sewer that followed us across the swamp, the trash floating by, or the two wild dogs that sulked pitifully around the grounds. What gave me pause was the fact that her house was all by itself; it was completely isolated.

I couldn't speak for all of Kenya, but in the urban slums I'd visited, people seemed to live communally. The houses—made of sticks, mud, galvanized iron, or timber, depending on which village you found yourself in—were always close together. Some were literally connected, the walls on either side shared with the neighbor next door. Others had space in between them—be it inches or meters—but were still lined up in a row as if to prove their solidarity. Then there were some that were more scattered and less orderly but close enough to each other to share a central latrine, a clothesline, or an enclosure for chickens.

There was something about this house that felt different, even ominous. We had journeyed down uneven dirt paths and through thickly populated slums to get to this swamp, where we were scheduled to meet Pamela.

The house was tiny and made of mabati, or dull iron sheets. The pitched roof, also made of metal sheets, looked like it might blow away with a strong gust of wind. There were two cutouts on either side of the doorframe that should have been windows, but they were boarded up with thin slats of wood that didn't allow much light or air in—or out. Around the base of the house was a barricade of small rocks, maybe intended to keep the swamp water out, although I doubted they did their job.

After what felt like an hour's trek through ankle-deep standing water, the six of us walked to Pamela's door. I lifted my arm to knock but stopped when Cornel told me, "Just walk in. She never has visitors, so she knows it could only be us."

The house was a single room that was dim, musty, and sparse inside. I only saw a small couch, an upside-down box with an empty drinking glass on top of it, and a circle of rocks in the corner, which I assumed was used for a cooking fire. I thought no one was home until I saw movement on the couch. From under a blanket, a figure slowly turned to face us. She managed to perch herself up onto her elbow but was too listless to sit up all the way. Cornel and Duncan went to her side and encouraged her into a sitting position. They draped the blanket over her lap as she thanked them softly and looked at the four of us standing shyly in the corner.

Cornel introduced us by name and then said, "My friends, please meet Pamela."

The woman who sat before us was skin and bones; she looked like she might break if she breathed too deeply. Her skin was covered in white blotches, as though she had third-degree burns from head to toe that were in different stages of healing—fresh, bleeding, infected, scabbed, and scarred. Her eyes lingered at half-mast, which didn't look like a sign of sleepiness as much as it did sadness, like she didn't have the will to open them any wider. Her hair was very short in some places and absent in others, small tufts resembling how I thought a cancer patient's might during the early stages of chemotherapy. Her lips were cracked and colored with dried blood, and her voice hoarse.

Cornel translated from Luo to English as we asked her questions on camera. We talked to her about her upbringing, her faith, the sequence of events that led her to where she was, and her thoughts about the future. A sadness inhabited her. I didn't see it just in her eyes but also in her whole being. I sensed it in every movement and every sound.

I'd seen and heard some hard things in the previous weeks—conversations and images that sat in the pit of my stomach as if an internal fist were clinging to them for dear life. But for some reason, the sight of Pamela—the physical manifestation of her virus, the stereotypical circumstances of an unfaithful husband infecting his faithful wife, the utter isolation in which she was now forced to live—hit me hardest of all. She was a woman who'd been handed a death sentence with no hope of pardon. Her life was disintegrating in front of my eyes.

It's been over a decade since that trip to Kenya, which feels like a long time and like no time at all. Since then, I've gone back to Africa more times than I can count, and much of what I've seen still sits in the pit of my stomach—the pain, the joy, the injustice, the progress, the devastation, and the restoration have all become part of me and part of the extraordinary journey that I never saw coming. None of us could have even imagined it. To this day, Cornel, Duncan, and I are still in awe of all that's transpired.

We're honored to tell the story that fills the following pages. It's told by all three of us, which is fitting, since each of us was as important as the other in what took place. It's a reflection of how we view our partnership, which goes beyond business and even friendship to form a brotherhood—two Kenyans and one American who had nothing in common until they had everything in common.

# CHAPTER ONE

# CORNEL

I began walking at eight months. Not just walking but running. My mother will tell you that on the very day I took my first steps, I also chased her through the market as she went to go fetch something. She already had my eldest brother, Leonard, by then. He had not walked until he was thirteen months, so she knew to be surprised. Yes, to hear her tell it, *nodhii mabor*, he was going places.

I grew up in the village of Seka Kagwa, in Kendu Bay. It is just outside the Kenyan port city of Kisumu. My home was no more than a hundred yards from Lake Victoria, the second-largest freshwater lake in the world. My tribe is Luo, and we are a tribe of fishermen. For centuries, we have relied on the lake to catch fish like tilapia, Nile perch, and omena to eat and sell. But from a young age, despite netting fish for shillings as early as ten years old, I knew I did not want to grow up to be a fisherman. The problem was that there was not a lot of opportunity to be something more.

My mother and father were not educated. Neither of them even made it through primary school. Because of that, or maybe in spite of it, I was determined to go as far as I could. I eagerly waited for the day I could finally lift my right arm up over my head and touch the bottom of my left ear with my hand. That was the sign that one was old enough to attend school. If you try it on a child of three or four years, they cannot do it. I have met Westerners who are shocked to hear of that measure of growth. But, you see, most children in my village did not know how old they were. We were born at home so we did not have birth certificates. We were born to illiterate mothers so no date of birth was known or written down.

As each of my seven brothers and sisters passed the hand-to-ear test, they too began attending school. I am happy to report that each of us completed primary school, all the way from class 1 to class 8. But we were only able to do so because it was free. There were only a few small charges here and there for uniforms and books. As small as those costs were, it was still a miracle that we were able to pay them at all.

We did not have any money. But we did not know anyone who did, so I never felt too sorry about it as a boy. Lake Victoria was once a rich source of income for the bordering countries of Kenya, Uganda, and Tanzania. But it became overfished. Too many fishermen were all trying to catch the same thing. And the amount of available fish was always shrinking. In the 1950s, in order to boost that amount, several non-native fish were put into the lake. Nile perch were one of them. But they turned out to be predators who pushed our local fish further toward extinction. Many of those local fish had been algae-eating fish. When they were no longer around, the algae rapidly spread and ended up choking the lake. So did the water hyacinth. It may be nice to look at, with its green glossy leaves and purple flowers. But it is an aggressive weed. It sits on top of the water and restricts the oxygen of everything below it. It is crazy to think how one living thing can ravage an entire population.

The lack of livelihood around me served as proof that fishing was not my future. It encouraged me to become even more diligent about my studies. I ran home every day after school to make sure I had enough time before the sun went down to complete my work. Most days, there were upward of fifty assignments to do. We all knew what the teachers would do if they were not turned in. Or worse, done incorrectly. My mother told me I could wait to do it later by candlelight, as that was when my cousins and siblings usually did it. But the candlelight made me feel limited. Like I would not be able to properly absorb the information. Only once the sunlight was gone and my work was complete would I go outside to join the end of a football game, find food in nearby trash piles before they were set on fire, or walk down to the lake to bathe.

It was during those evening hours at the lake when I saw local fishermen meeting with different women. The light of the moon allowed me to see that the women were not their wives. They went together behind the bushes. When the women came back out, they carried fish. Sometimes more than two or three in each hand. I did not understand what was going on at that young age, of course. But I knew how hungry we all were. I knew that desperation sometimes created reckless behavior.

Those were the nights I tried to bathe as quickly as possible. I did not want to risk the fishermen telling my father that I did not know how to mind my own business. I hurried back home to get ready for bed. When it came time to sleep, I gathered with all of my siblings in the single room we shared. There was space on the floor for one mat made of papyrus leaves. All of us could fit if we lay vertically and promised not to toss or turn. There was one blanket among us. But we rarely needed it. One of the good things about a mud-brick home was that it stayed a pleasant temperature despite the heat of the dry season or the chill of the wet season.

Roosters and egrets always announced the rising sun, although

I often woke before their calls. My mother said it was because I was *koso kwe* and *gombo ng'eyo*, restless and curious. I escaped the house as quietly as I could to collect branches for firewood or to fill pots with lake water in case we had millet to boil. We did not have cows, only what was given as a dowry to nearby relatives. But I went around before school and offered to milk any cow that I saw. In return, I asked the owners if I could take some of the milk home. Sometimes they let me.

School was several kilometers away. My siblings tended to walk ahead, while I waited in front of Harrison's house each morning. He was my best friend. He and his family lived across from us, just down the hill toward the lake. Out of everyone in our class, only Harrison liked school as much as I did. His only downfall was that he ran late. We would have to hurry to catch up with the rest of the students. We made our way down the long stretch of dirt road to join the sea of green uniform shorts, white collared shirts, bare feet, and books. Most of us did not have backpacks so we held our books. Even if I had a backpack, I would still have held my books in my hands. That was how you treated treasured items. I looked forward to school each day. It felt to me like an escape, although many would tell you it felt more like imprisonment.

But it was often more like hell than heaven because of the brutal spankings. I do not remember going one day without being hit. If you did, then you were among the luckiest. We did not necessarily get hit because we behaved badly. The punishment was more about power than discipline. The teachers seemed to enjoy it and delivered beatings for a great many things. If we did not complete our homework, we got spanked. If we missed a question on a test, we got spanked. Answer by answer, the teacher made us raise our hand if we got it wrong.

We were spanked with tree branches on our buttocks or back. Our uniforms were often faded and torn in those areas. We were also struck on the palm of the hand. Some teachers struck four times. Some struck twenty. It was not uncommon for students to bleed or faint. Some were taken to the hospital. The parents accepted these actions. No one questioned a teacher. They were held in high esteem. There was no way a teacher was wrong. Students were to obey and endure any punishment the teacher gave, period.

There were times we tried to outsmart the teachers by putting books between our buttocks and our shorts so we would not feel it when they hit us. That was soon discovered due to the sound of the stroke against the hardcover of the textbook. We then cut out thin layers of mattress and sewed them into our underwear to provide padding. When that was also discovered, we were made to strip off our shorts and underwear in front of the whole school during the weekly parade. They hit us on our bare behinds in what was as painful as it was humiliating. For many kids, the treatment was too much to bear. Many ran away from school. Some never returned. I always returned. The beatings were the cost of learning.

My favorite subject was English. Our national language was Swahili, of course, although most in our village spoke only Luo. Those of us at school were privileged to learn English as well. I spent hours studying English grammar and was fascinated by the way the words were constructed. I was eager for ways to practice. The school did not have any books for us to read besides government-issued textbooks that we shared in school only, so I would go to indoor markets looking for brochures and magazines. I often read aloud to people passing by.

I believe it was in those articles that I first learned of the science behind HIV/AIDS. For years, there had been talk in our village about a disease that caused many deaths. Most of the people affected seemed to be women. At least, that was what the men said. No one spoke of the disease by name. It seemed there was no need since the physical signs were obvious enough. A woman got very skinny. And then she got kicked out of her home. That meant she had it. There was no need to discuss it further. Doing so might spread the *chira*, the curse. But as I learned more about the disease, I knew the silence was about much more than the fear of a curse. It was that people could not speak about what they did not understand.

If the articles sparked my interest in AIDS, my curiosity caught fire at school. We took health class during the later years of primary school and received quite a bit of information about it. Since most of the material was in English, I imagined that the Western world was full of only scientists and doctors. I remember thinking how unfair it was that those of us hearing the truth about AIDS were not the people who needed to hear it most. We as youth were not in a position to change minds or abolish shame. I felt trapped because what I learned could not go beyond me. I could not speak of it in the village and did not dare bring it up at home. Where I came from, the secret to survival was knowing your place.

Especially with my father. He was a stern man. He was in charge of what we spoke about and what we believed. He expected to be served and respected. He enforced discipline. He had the final say in family matters. It was all very typical of Luo culture. Men were *wuon dala*, head of the homestead. I imagine his father was the same way, although I did not know him. My father did not know him either. He died when my father was only three years old. My father was quick to anger. Perhaps it stemmed from that. No father and too much *changaa*, homebrew.

Although not in a physical sense, my grandfather was still very present in our lives. Many members from my father's side of the family lived on my grandfather's land with us, another thing typical of Luos. I grew up with my aunts, uncles, and cousins all within shouting distance. It was a village within a village. We all had mud and stick homes with grass-thatched roofs. We all had a separate outdoor mud-brick room to use as a kitchen. We all had latrines made from branches of *Markhamia lutea*, the Nile tulip. We were spaced out just enough to make us feel both independent and connected with each other.

One of my first cousins and his wife lived a five-minute walk away. They were the farthest out from the rest of us. Their placement afforded them more privacy. But we were still aware of their comings and goings. We noticed right away when my cousin started leaving his wife for weeks at a time.

A cultural practice of our tribe is wife inheritance. That means when a male relative dies and leaves behind a wife, a member of his family must inherit her. The ancient custom was meant to ensure that the widow had someone to support her and her children financially and to carry on the family lineage. It was also a way to keep her late husband's wealth within the family bloodline. The new husband therefore provides for her but does not need to move her into his home. He goes back and forth from one home and wife to another. That was why my cousin was gone for long stretches. It turned out that a distant relative in a nearby village had passed on. My cousin was with his inherited wife and her children.

I knew that polygamy and wife inheritance had long been part of our culture. But that was the first time someone in my family had practiced it in front of my eyes. I figured the adults would be pleased that my cousin upheld such a time-honored tradition. Instead, it was met with grave concern. I overheard them discussing how the distant relative died suspiciously. He was *odhero ahinya*, rail thin, and had the look. They said his widow had also lost a great deal of weight in recent months. They spoke about the need to cleanse our land. And then I heard my grandmother say that the inherited wife was rumored to be a Kikuyu. That caused the biggest gasps. Out of the forty-plus tribes in Kenya, Luo and Kikuyu had the most rivalry. Still, I was surprised to hear that her being Kikuyu could have been more tragic than having a deadly disease.

My father's eldest brother put a stop to everything. He decided that my cousin just needed to keep up his part of the land. Beyond that, they were not to concern themselves with rumors. And that was that. Life continued.

As the fishing trade got worse, more and more people were out of work. My father was one of them, although I do not really remember a time when he was regularly trying to catch fish in the first place. He did not go down to the lake each day with the other fishermen. He did not spend the hour before sunset bleeding the fish and removing their guts. He rarely brought home money. I knew that because I heard my parents discussing it. My mother would ask if she could have a couple shillings to get flour or beans at the market, and my father would hit her and tell her, "Ionge erokamano," "You are ungrateful."

In our culture, the role of the woman was *tiyo gi luor*, to serve and obey. They stayed quiet. They raised the children, cooked for the family, cleaned the home, and grew basic staple crops. But as my father continued to not work, my mother took on more responsibility. She wove baskets out of papyrus reeds with my sisters and took them to the Oriang market, in Kendu Bay, every Thursday. She taught herself how to make jewelry and then washed merchants' clothes in exchange for beads and hardware. She went down to the lakeshore and tried to catch sardines with a net or with a pole and hook if someone lent her one. Since she did not have access to a boat and could not swim, she was limited to walking out waist-deep and hoping the fish were not scared off by the movement of her legs. What little money she made went toward school uniforms and food. It was understandable that when it came time to pay for our secondary school, there was nothing left.

Once a Kenyan student completes class 8, they must pass a national examination in order to attend secondary school. It is highly stressful for the pupils. Some start studying months in advance. Some stay late at school to review textbooks. Some lie awake for hours at night going over multiplication tables in their head. Those of us who took great pride in academia did all of those things. I did not just want to pass. I wanted to pass with the best possible score so I could gain admission to the best possible secondary school.

Secondary lasts four years, similar to an American high school. There are three types of government-funded secondary schools one could go to based on the outcome of their exams: national, provincial, or district. Students with the highest scores got into national schools. That is what everyone strove for. They were better schools that provided a better chance of getting into university. They were even rumored to have things like laboratory equipment, musical instruments, and sports gear. The problem was that they were the most expensive out of the three types of schools. The student not only paid for a better academic experience. They also paid to live on campus. These were not day schools but boarding schools. So even though the government paid for a large part of it, there were high boarding costs that the family was responsible to cover. Upward of 32,000 shillings, or around US$320, per year.

There was a four-year age gap between my brother Leonard and me. He trailed behind in primary school. I sped ahead, so we finished class 8 and took the examination at the same time. I was very anxious during the long month of waiting for results. Leonard did not seem affected. Even on the day we received notice that the results were in, he chose not to walk to the school to find out. "Nyisa duoko na kiduogo," "Just tell me my results when you get back," he said.

Harrison and I ran to school and stood with the crowd outside the head teacher's door. The list was posted. My legs trembled as I jumped up and down from the back to try to spot any information I could. When I saw a clearing, I elbowed my way in and traced my finger down until I found my name. Next to it was my score. I opened and shut my eyes to make sure I saw it correctly. My scores were high. High enough to make me eligible for admission to a national school. A sense of honor rushed over me, stronger than anything I had felt before. I knew then the true value of *sinani*, perseverance.

Leonard's score made him eligible to attend a provincial school. Harrison scored highest out of us three. We spent the walk home discussing which national school we would attend together. My mother and father were very proud when I shared the news. Their two eldest sons had passed the national examination.

It was an unseasonably cold and wet afternoon several weeks later when my mother sat me and Leonard down to confirm what we knew but did not want to admit: She could not afford to send us to school. At least, not both of us. And certainly not to a national or provincial school. She told us that she may be able to provide a little money for one of us, but it would have to be a district school. The closest one was in Kisumu, seventy kilometers away. And that would still only work if the rest of the fees were earned and paid by the son who chose to attend.

Leonard and I looked at each other. I nodded. He was the eldest. He should be the one to go. I opened my mouth to tell him so right as he stood up, extended his hand, and said, "In ema idhi," "You should attend."

I had long known that Leonard did not have the passion I did for education. At times, I felt it was my elevated level of enthusiasm that pushed us both through primary. He often complained about going and seemed content just staying around the house. Even though I was not the same way, I understood. School was hard in every way. The struggle to comprehend the teachings was often the least of it. For as many could not afford the fees, just as many could not afford the pain.

I asked Leonard several times if he was sure. He nodded and repeated, "An somba ogik gi ka," "Yes I will sit back." The look in his eye was of pure relief.

I began working any job I could find. I mixed mortar and pushed wheelbarrows at small construction sites. I pedaled a bicycle taxi and drove a *boda boda*, a motorcycle taxi. I dug graves for the growing number of funerals each weekend. I cooked and served food in a *kibanda*, a restaurant. I slowly saved up 5,000 shillings. It may have been only a little money. But to me, it was a whole world. I knew it was not close to covering even the initial registration fee. But I felt it was enough to show the school I was serious about learning. It would serve as a sign of trust that I would continue to pay.

Standard practice was that the head of the household enrolled their student in secondary. The adult was to visit the school, state the intention of their child to attend, and pay some or all of the registration and tuition. I went to my father and gave him all my shillings. It was time for him to enroll me at Bar Union High School, in Kisumu Nyahera, I told him proudly. He said he would.

Later that morning, I stood in the doorway of our home and watched him walk in the direction of the school with the money in his pocket. I stayed awake as long as I could that night, waiting for him to return to tell me how it went. By the next morning, he was still not home.

I finally saw my father some days later. He told me in Luo, "Oh, my son, those school people think you are great. They are so happy. Those people will now send you a calling letter."

A week went by. Nothing came from the school. I arrived home from one of my jobs as my father stumbled out the front doorway.

"Just wait. They are coming. Be patient, my son," he said as he walked by me without looking.

After more weeks passed, my mother mentioned that a distant aunt, called Prisca, worked as an accountant at Bar Union. That was all I needed to hear. I took off on foot to go check with the school myself. I was met with happiness from my aunt when she saw me but sadness when she checked with the secretary and confirmed that the school had never heard of me. My father had not gone to the school to enroll me. I knew the money had been long spent.

I allowed myself to feel disappointed and betrayed only during the walk back home. Once I arrived, my determination to go to secondary school took over. My mother gently told me I should not expect to go. There was no way to pay for it. I had rarely, if ever, gone against my mother's advice. But that time, I insisted that she let me go. I would work. I would find food. I would find shelter.

She paused and said, "Abiro dhi kodi," "I will go with you." She managed to borrow 5,000 shillings from her friends. We used part of it to pay for public transportation to Kisumu, where we traveled with one shared bag of clothes and belongings. We put the other part toward the school fee. I had missed the first two months of the three-month term. But they allowed me to enroll as long as I kept up payments. Aunt Prisca played a big role in this. I will never forget that kindness.

My mother was hopeful she could find more small business opportunities in Kisumu than in Seka. While I stayed with an aunt called Margret who lived close to the school, my mother rented a small wooden shack in the slums of Nyalenda as she worked hard to save money. Back and forth she went from the slum to our village. She put shillings toward my schooling and then took some back home to pay the fees for my brothers and sisters still in primary school. She supplied small bits of food for me and then took food back for my father and siblings. It was as if she lived a double life. My father was not pleased. Each time she went back to Seka, he would scream that she did not know her place. She needed to stay and take care of him, the home, and the other children. She eventually headed back to Kisumu but for shorter and shorter periods of time, always with fresh bruises.

I worked on and off that entire first year of secondary. I would attend classes for some weeks and then work a job for some weeks. Most of what I found was maintenance work in restaurants. It not only supplied me with a little money for fees but also with a little food. I would wait until the restaurant closed each night and then sort through the trash to find discarded scraps. The weeks I attended school were filled with hunger.

But all of that ended when the school administrator officially sent me away. He said I owed too much money. I could not return for the second year until my first year was paid in full. I went seventy kilometers back to Seka, determined to find another solution.

It was wonderful to see my family after such a long time away. I had never been gone that long before. I also enjoyed visiting many of my friends with whom I had attended primary school. The majority had not gone on to secondary school despite passing exams. The common reason was money, although it did not just pertain to school fees. The larger issue for many of them was having to cover the cost of household provisions.

There had been a high increase in deaths over those years. Many of my age-mates had mothers and fathers who had passed on or were so ill they were close to it. My fellow teenagers therefore had to make ends meet for their brothers and sisters. They stepped into the role of parent and provider. Some of the males became fishermen. Some of the females made and sold crafts like pottery or reed mats. I am sad to say that some were unable to find work because of their association with the HIV virus.

The village had far more abandoned homes than when I left. They were boarded up so as not to let the chira out into the wind. Many of the children or surviving spouses who used to live there had been shunned and sent away to live with relatives. Others built makeshift homes on the outskirts of town. Some orphans relied on the compassion of the rare few who would care for someone with such direct association with the disease.

There was a home on our family land that was boarded up as well. My cousin, the one who inherited the wife, had passed away several months prior to my return. The initial concern from the adults in my family had been warranted. He contracted HIV from his inherited wife. In turn, he infected his first wife. She then birthed two children who were both born with it. My cousin and both his wives died within mere weeks of one another. The children were dispersed among family outside Seka. My father said it was for protection. I don't know if he was referring to the children or our family. I felt sick to my stomach either way.

The village felt heavy. Like it was suffocating under the weight of the disease, like the lake under the hyacinths. I knew just the person who could help lift my spirits: Harrison. I had not seen him since before I left for Kisumu the year before. I walked over to his house. His mother greeted me in the doorway. I asked if he was home. She extended her arm inside but did not say anything. I went in and found him lying on a small mattress in the corner of the room. He rose up to his elbows when he saw me. His sunken face and skinny arms told me all I needed to know. I went over to him and fell to my knees. It was one of the last times I would see him alive.

It got so bad so fast. The spread of AIDS devastated my village, like gasoline thrown on a wildfire. Maybe the chaos was there all along. Maybe it was just the acknowledgment of the disease that spread. Maybe the polygamy and impulsive behavior of fishermen were finally met with consequence. Maybe my time away allowed me to come back with fresh eyes and see what had been hidden in plain sight the whole time. Maybe the state of our village was the new normal.

I was not around too much longer to find out. I received word that a harambee school had opened in Kisumu. Americans would call that a charter school. It was in the slum where my mother had stayed and was the first of its kind in the area. Since it was just starting, they had nothing, only two teachers, Mr. Sila and Mr. Anguka, and no books, desks, aides, or supplies. They also had no tuition. Any small costs associated with the school were ten times cheaper than the cheapest district school in Kenya. That is how I became the thirty-third student ever at Kassagam High School.

The school struggled due to the lack of resources. As a means of support, it became sponsored by a local church. I was into my third year when that happened. Members of the church started coming every Thursday for Christian Union. They met with students to share about the Christian faith and hand out tracts so we could study different books of the Bible. Spiritual nourishment, they called it. I went to a Catholic church here and there growing up. My family was not consistent in our attendance and did not often speak about our beliefs at home. It was not until Kassagam that I was formally introduced to Christianity.

The school became Kassagam Baptist High School. And I became a Christian. I began to read the Bible daily and learned more and more about the life of Christ. As I did, something filled up inside me that I had not known was empty. I felt as though I finally had somewhere to place my grief and fears. I had someone to help shoulder the hopelessness and sorrow I felt about the conditions of my village. The pain of watching loved ones like Harrison die at the hands of others' decisions. The injustice of my brothers and sisters struggling to attend school. The hardships my mother endured at the hands and fists of my father. The demons my father battled at the expense of his family. The frustration of wanting more than what society told me was attainable. For the first time in my life, I was able to trade those burdens for weightless faith.

Like I had at Bar Union, I shifted between going to school and going to work. Some weeks here and some weeks there. Even though my presence was not as consistent as the other students, I was given the honor of class secretary. They placed me in that leadership position for all of my three years at Kassagam. It was a role I greatly valued. Reminiscent of my days as a debating prefect in class 6 and the school librarian in class 7, I enjoyed the responsibility, although the elite role did little to increase my chances of educational success.

I did not pass the secondary school examination at the end of my fourth year. None of the Kassagam students did. It was not surprising as much as it was disappointing. At a school like that, with very little to offer students in the way of academic support, it was expected that no one would pass. Where other schools held three-day rehearsals prior to the exam, we were shown some laboratory test examples one day before the exam. Where other schools had practical lessons as part of everyday learning, we were left to imagine how to use a computer keyboard, pipet, test tubes, Bunsen burner, or chemistry beaker. Our school was not even a registered exam center yet. The unfortunate consequence of all those factors meant we failed the very exam required for entry to university.

A poor person cannot afford to attend a good school. A poor school cannot equip students for academic success. A good student at a poor school only gains entry to a system that later locks them out. I left Kassagam, clinging to the promise that when God shuts a window, He opens a door. And that is precisely what happened.

# CHAPTER TWO

# DUNCAN

The head teacher did not slap me hard enough to make my nose bleed. Luckily, I had a weird condition back in those days where I could just rub my nose, and it would start bleeding. With the sound of the slap still ringing in the ears of the rest of the school children, I lifted my hand and quickly rubbed my nose from side to side. It worked just as I hoped. Blood began to drip as a look of shock crossed the teacher's face. Shock turned to remorse.

"Go home. I am sorry, my son."

He did not feel bad about hitting me, only that it resulted in blood. It was beyond what he expected to do. I did what he said and went home, arriving out of breath, with the front of my white uniform shirt covered in dried blood. My mother was there and slow to rise from her position in the garden. As she walked toward me, she did not look as worried as a mother should look when seeing her son in such a state. Instead, she looked suspicious, and her eyes asked, "What did you do this time?" I knew then that she was not going to believe whatever story I came up with.

"What teacher did this to you?" she asked me in Swahili.

I told her it was the same teacher who had been angry with me yesterday.

"Good. I will give him a chicken," she said in Kikuyu.

Uh-oh. It was never a good sign when my mother mixed languages.

"You are not even going to ask me what happened?"

"I will let your father ask you," she said, sticking with Kikuyu.

I prepared myself for the long night ahead. I knew what would happen when he got home, because it was the same thing that happened every time he got home and had to hear about my poor decisions, as he called them. He would open his Bible and quote Hebrews 13:17: "Obey your leaders and submit to them, for they are keeping watch over your souls, as those who will have to give an account. Let them do this with joy and not with groaning, for that would be of no advantage to you." There was no need for him to open the Bible. He did not read from it. He knew the verse by heart. We all did. I think he just did it for show, and I will admit that it was very effective. There was something humbling about a pastor standing before you with an open Bible in one hand and reasonable expectations in the other.

He would spend the next hour sharing with me parables about the importance of respecting authority. Hezekiah did not get angry when Sennacherib tried to turn the Israelite people against God but instead remained silent and prayed. Nehemiah respected King Artaxerxes enough to ask him permission to rebuild the wall around Jerusalem. Elisha traveled to Bethel, and when the boys from town made fun of his bald head, God sent two bears to attack all forty-two of the boys who had teased him. These one-sided discussions would end in prayer, followed by my promise to stop getting into trouble. But despite my best intentions, drama seemed to follow me wherever I went. It had followed me to Gitura. That was for sure.

We moved around a lot when I was very young. I was born in

Meru, near Mt. Kenya, but my father's work as a pastor meant we traveled to any church that needed him. That turned out to be a lot of churches in a lot of towns. By the time I reached seven years old, we had landed in a village outside Nakuru by the name of Gitura, and my father decided it was time to put down roots. It was a big village, with around 350 other families, but the land was so vast we never would have guessed there were that many people. All we saw were fields.

The Kikuyu were originally hunter-gatherers, but we gradually adopted horticultural practices. That is a fancy way of saying we are a tribe of farmers. Most live in the highlands, about 200 kilometers east of Lake Victoria, on red earth soil perfect for growing cash crops like coffee and tea. Cash crops do not necessarily translate to cash. It just means they are grown to sell rather than to feed the grower's livestock or family. The average farmer in my village worked from sunrise to sunset just to be able to sell enough to survive the next day, and many could not even do that.

We were among those who pulled off daily miracles. Although my father worked as a pastor his entire adult life, it was an unpaid position. Local church officials did not make any money, since the communities they served did not have any money to give. Apart from one or two people in our village who had proper jobs like a teacher or policeman, nobody had formal employment. My father used to say he was paid in souls saved. In reality, he was paid in eggs, milk, and beans. His parishioners gifted him food when they had a small surplus after harvest or an overproducing cow or chicken.

Our own land provided us with some food, but we focused more on selling it than eating it. We had half an acre where we grew coffee, maize, and sweet potatoes, and we also had avocado and citrus trees. My mother and sisters walked to town twice a week to sell what we had harvested the week before. They were meager earnings, but our basic needs were met. We had somewhere to sleep and something to eat. We did not buy clothes, we did not have presents for Christmastime, we did not have running water or electricity, but we did not know anyone who did.

Our biggest luxury was that we attended school. With seven children in one house, the cost for uniforms, books, supplies, and examinations added up quickly. I have an older brother and sister, three younger brothers, and a last-born sister. We were all two years apart from one another, which meant that once my mother and father were done paying for one child's schooling, there was always another in waiting. I did not know until many years later that they often relied on the goodwill of people in our community to spare a shilling here or bank note there. That was why my father was swift in his correction of our behavior when it came to school. He saw it as being disrespectful not just to the teachers but also to the neighbors who helped support our schooling.

I did not consider myself disrespectful. I was outgoing and perhaps a little impulsive. My intention was never to be rude. I only wanted to make people laugh. That was why the nosebleed situation happened in the first place.

It all started on the day prior to my teacher slapping me. All the class 6 students were sitting in our classroom when the teacher asked us to each donate one shilling to help fund a new school being built nearby.

I felt it was a silly request. None of the students had any money, and it was likely that our mothers and fathers did not have any either. Especially not one whole shilling extra, just lying around.

I whispered to the students around me, "Do they think we dig in the ground and find money?"

The teacher turned to look in my direction.

"Duncan, do you have something to say?"

I sat there, silent.

He looked at my desk mate and asked him to repeat what I said, and he did.

"Did you say that, Duncan?"

I looked down and did not respond.

"Duncan, come here."

I did not move. As the teacher approached my desk, I reached to my right and grabbed one of the wooden slats that formed the classroom wall. Each classroom was made of old wood. Whoever built them put the planks in a vertical pattern with a good inch or two of space between each one. It allowed water to come in when it rained and heat to come in when it was dry, which I hated because sitting right next to the wall made me a victim of the elements. But on that day, I was grateful. Those inches of space allowed me to stick my fingers through and pull one of the planks toward me. I heard it split from the above support beam, and then I threw it to my right. That was my mistake. It could have hit someone. I squeezed my body sideways through the new gap in the wall and took off running.

"Get him!" the teacher yelled. That was his mistake.

Some other classes were outside on break, and they turned to see the disturbance coming from our classroom. When the students saw me run, many began to run after me. My classmates, having been instructed to chase me, also began to run after me. Soon, every student in the entire school was running after me. I ran beyond the school grounds and onto a nearby coffee plantation. The students followed, all 300 of them. I ran through the rows of crop, darting in and out so they would have trouble spotting me. I did not stop running until I arrived home, where I unleashed a dog tied to our fence post. The dog chased the children back into the plantation. What a good diversion! At last, there was no one left behind me.

My mother was not there. But when she got home hours later, the look on her face told me she already knew what happened.

The whole village knew what happened, because all of the children arrived home from school early due to my careless and cheeky behavior. That was what the teacher called it.

The day after that was the slapping incident. I wish it had ended there, but on the third day, I was sent to the office as soon as I got to school. The headmaster asked me to apologize for my actions over the last two days, which I did. He then held me by the waist and removed my shorts. My bottom half was as naked as the day I was born. He told me to follow him out onto the dirt field, where the morning parade had already begun. He took my shorts and placed them in the center of the dirt, right in the middle of the large circle of students and teachers. Everyone stopped and stared. The headmaster did not tell me to go get my shorts. He did not have to. I knew I had no choice but to run as fast as I could to grab them and put them on while everyone pointed and laughed. I was humiliated, which was the point, but I would have pointed and laughed too if it had been someone else, so of course I did not fault them. Still, it was enough to make me not want to show my face for the rest of the day, so I ran home. Again.

It ended the next day. My mother and father marched me right into the office and asked the headmaster to forgive my discretions and asked whether we could please put all of this behind us. He agreed, which I am sure was because my father was his pastor. The three of them looked at me like they wanted a final apology, which I gave. My father then asked me to be serious about my studies and to show appreciation for the blessing of education. I told him I would, and I mostly meant it.

The next few years looked a lot like the ones before it, although I tried to balance my bad with good. I took apart my father's radio when I knew I was not supposed to touch it. I ran away from home with my friends to try to get out of sitting for our class 8 examinations. I took my father's bicycle despite the strict rule that we were not allowed to ride it. Then I spent one of my school breaks building a pen for some goats we had been given. I spent another break tilling my aunt's field with a mattock. I spent yet another sitting in an isolated shed for a month after undergoing our tribal custom of circumcision. I told my father someone should redefine the term "break," and he quoted Proverbs 12:24: "Diligent hands will rule, but laziness ends in forced labor."

That was around the time I began secondary school. My older brother and sister already attended. In fact, my brother was in his final year. My father was so proud. For as long as I could remember, he had preached to us the importance of education and of his commitment to providing for it. There was a tinge of regret in his voice when he spoke of school. We all sensed it, and we all knew where it came from.

My father grew up in a polygamous family, and my grandfather had a total of four wives and twelve children. He worked as a slave for a wealthy British family, and in return, they housed all of his wives and children in the backwoods of their estate. One night, my grandfather was caught stealing kerosene from a storage shed, which was against the rules, because slaves were not allowed luxuries like light or warmth.

The next day, the British patriarch asked my grandfather to gather all of his wives and children to accompany him on a walk. My grandfather did as he was asked, and they followed the owner around the property until they came to a large hole in the ground. No one had ever seen it there before. Suddenly, a gunshot rang out, and my grandfather fell face-first into the hole. He had been shot in the back. The British man told the wives and children to cover the body with the mound of dirt that was piled next to the hole. Then, each of the four wives was sent away in a separate direction, on foot, with only their children and the clothes on their back. My father and uncle were sent east with their now-single mother.

During that time, being unmarried with children was a source of shame. It did not matter the circumstances. Even today, that stigma remains among certain tribes. My grandmother remained unwed and devoted her time to finding work and raising her sons. It was a hard life. Even though she found occasional work, it was not enough to provide her sons with opportunities like school. With their futures limited, my father found refuge in his faith, and my uncle became a freedom fighter. The chances of ever having education and money were buried with my grandfather that day, and I feel my father has been trying to make up for it ever since.

When school fees were due, especially once we reached secondary, where the costs were much higher than primary, my father sold many of his belongings. His best shovels, his beloved radio, his Sunday shoes. My siblings and I had always helped our parents by working the land and helping with chores, but now we searched for outside work to earn real wages. I found a job, which I loved, selling newspapers. The newspaper vendor would hand you a pile for free, and you earned a commission from whatever you sold that day. I tried to be as entertaining as I could while standing at bus stops and shops. Through God's grace and my good charm, I was able to pay for one whole term with the money I earned. That was at the end of my first year, but after that, it got much more complicated.

I remember waking up in the middle of the night with a pain in my stomach. At first, I did not know where I was. The darkness confused me. My entire body felt hot even though I was on the cool dirt floor of the bedroom. Was our home on fire? I reached out to touch the timber wall. It was cold to touch, and I inched my way over and rested my face against it. That was when I realized how much my stomach hurt. It was a sharp pain, what I imagined getting stabbed felt like. I hoped the feeling would pass and tried to distract myself by praying until I saw sunlight come through the rafters of our tin roof. I gently called for my mother, barely above a whisper. At first, I was so quiet because I did not want to disturb my sleeping siblings, but then it was because I could not raise my voice. Doing so meant I would have needed to take a deep breath, and anything beyond a shallow inhale hurt too much. Was there something wrong with my lungs?

My mother took one look at me and decided we needed to go see a doctor. The closest clinic was six kilometers away, but I could hardly walk. I was having trouble even standing up straight. My mother bent over and told me to get on her back. I told her, no, I would break her bones if I did, but she insisted. I never would have thought my mother was capable of lifting me, and even if she could, I would not have thought she was able to walk more than a few steps. But she did. She carried me on her back the entire six kilometers.

We were seen quickly at the clinic. Not in a prompt way but in a careless way. The doctor came in, took my temperature, shined a light in my eyes, and walked out. Then the nurse came in and told me I had malaria. My mother and I looked at each other, surprised. We had both had malaria before. So had every-one else in our family. So had every person in Kenya. This was not what malaria felt like. But who were we to disagree with the doctor? They wrote me a prescription for a high dose of malaria medication, told me to take it for six days, and sent me home.

I continued to feel horrible. The pain in my stomach contin-ued and started to spread to my back. In the village, they have this notion that the worse you react to the malaria medication, the better it is working. I hoped the village was right, that the medication was fighting what was wrong, and I just needed to stay strong. But for the next two weeks, I was still in severe pain. I had schoolwork to do and money to earn but, instead, spent day after day lying in a ball on the floor.

My father was home more than usual during those two weeks. They were doing repairs at the church so he held his weekly meetings in the main room of our home. With all of my siblings at school, there was not a lot for me to do, so I listened from one room away as my father met with different members of the congregation. Some people were there for counseling sessions, some for Bible readings, and some to plan funeral services. I heard all about the troubles men and women face when they are newly married, I heard in-depth discussions about two of the nine fruits of the spirit from Galatians, and I heard sobbing as two women prepared for the burial of their brother.

"We will be honest with you, Pastor," one of the women said. "He died of AIDS, but you cannot say that at his funeral. When you are conducting the service, you must say he died of malaria or tuberculosis."

My father told them how those who perished from AIDS were wrapped in a special bag before being placed into the ground. The material of the bag kept the disease from spreading into the soil and infecting the land. "So I must tell you," he said, "the mourners in attendance will know when they see the bag."

That led to more sobbing.

I cannot say that AIDS was often discussed openly. At least, not that I heard. Most people in the village who spoke of it called it mukingo, which translated to "weak neck." I assumed it got that name because the people who had it were very weak and thin. They seemed to be only bones. That word became attached to the person. Like, if I had AIDS, people would have referred to me as Duncan Mukingo. It was a way to brand people and assign the disease to them without speaking its actual name.

Once the women left, I heard my father talking to my mother about whether he should perform the service of the deceased brother. "It is a sinful disease," he said. "I do not want the church to be associated with it."

Listening through the wall, I thought of the Jesus in the ever-open Bible in my father's hand. Jesus, always touching lepers. Jesus, never looking away. I wondered if my father or the church would ever do the same for those with the "weak neck."

Those thoughts were swiftly driven out of my mind by pain. Something occurred in my stomach then, something that felt worse than before, which I did not think was possible. There was something very wrong, and we all knew it. We all also knew it was not malaria so it was decided that we had to get a second opinion. My mother and I boarded a matatu, a minibus, that very day and rode it all the way to a district hospital in Nakuru.

This doctor also seemed to be in a big rush when he came in. He also seemed very young, like he could have been a friend of my older brother. He read off a list of questions from a clipboard and wrote my answers without ever looking at me. He asked the nurse to do a blood test and then came back in and told me, "You do not have malaria."

"Yes, I know. What do I have?"

"There is something wrong with your intestines."

Could they tell that from a blood test?

"We will now prepare you for surgery," he said as he walked out.

I stayed in the hospital for several weeks after that surgery. They told me they found blood in my stomach area and had removed a part of my intestine that had probably been leaking. The problem was fixed, and I could go home soon. By the time I did, I felt better. The pain in my stomach was far less, and the scars on my skin were healing well.

I began attending secondary school again. I had been away for close to two months and did my best to catch up on all that I missed. My father was often at the school office, talking with them about payment. They knew he was a pastor, they knew pastors were not paid, and they knew we had to pay the hospital, so they gave me favor. The school fees were written as arrears, money owed, and I was allowed to continue with my studies. Every morning, my father gathered us together for prayer before school and praised the Lord for His blessings.

Over the next six months, I did well in school but began to struggle physically. It was not the pain in my stomach, which was now just a constant dull ache, but the rest of my body. I was tired from my head to my feet, would get very high fevers, and, some days, did not even have the strength to rise. Some days were better than others, of course. There were times when I felt almost normal and attended school or went into town to sell newspapers.

Still, it was an isolating time. On the days I was sick, it was not just that I was bored and by myself while my siblings were at school or playing outside. It was that no one could truly understand how I felt. My parents and siblings were patient with me, and I could tell they had sympathy, but they could not fully appreciate the pain of my body. They could not understand my guilt about missing school or not earning wages. They could not comprehend my sadness over the betrayal of my body.

Even though they had many responsibilities to tend to each day, my parents cared for me very well. My mother checked on me, urged me to eat, and, on my worst days, helped me bathe and visit the latrine. My father prayed over my body and read to me from the book of Romans. As he put it, "Romans shows us what God is like, how He saves us, and how He wants us to live."

What did sick people do when they did not have anyone to care for them? What would I have done had my mother and father not helped me? There was no way I could have survived. I was humbled by their support and found a deep appreciation I had not had before. I always knew they were loving and hardworking parents, but I began to see just how selfless, compassionate, and faithful they were as people.

I was back at the hospital in Nakuru one full year after my first stomach pain. A doctor saw me and used a machine to look at the insides of my stomach area. He said he wanted to do another operation, which he did later that day. Afterward, he came into my hospital room and told me I had suffered from something called appendicitis. That was why my stomach hurt all those months before. Those first doctors had not seen that my appendix was inflamed and that it had later burst. During my previous surgery, they cleaned up the infectious materials from the burst appendix and removed a section of my lower intestines, which they thought were to blame.

"If a doctor does not know to look at the appendix, that is an understandable course of action," the doctor said. "But the reason you have been ill all this time later is that they accidentally left a piece of cotton wool in your intestine during the procedure. Your abdominal cavity became very infected, and I had to remove parts of your intestine that had rotted."

It was a lot of medical terminology to use with simple people. I looked to my mother and father for guidance but they looked as confused as I did. The doctor saw it on our faces and said, "Duncan should be fine now. You can take him home in a few weeks' time."

I traveled back to Gitura with enough scars on my stomach to look like a map of Africa. The worst was over, but like any type of trauma, it took time to recover. And I do not just mean physically. Financially, it drained my parents completely. While I was sick, my firstborn brother finished secondary school and passed the final examination. He was due to go to university but could not because my parents now had to put all of their money toward the payment of my treatments. My father sold a piece of land, the only piece of land we had, to try to balance out the hospital costs, the arrears for both my sister and me at secondary, and the fees for my younger siblings at primary.

Emotionally, it was a time of both grief and growth. The last year had provided me with many hours to reflect on my humanity, my childish ways, the physical limitations of my body, and the blessing that my mother and father were to me. I spent time in prayer, thanking God that I was still alive and asking Him to turn me into who He wanted me to become. I carried with me a lot of guilt over the hardships my parents endured due to my illness and felt shame about the behavior of my youth. After all of the sacrifices they had made to send my siblings and me to school, my sneaky antics were not the proper way to say thank you. I asked for their forgiveness, and they further inspired me by the way they freely gave it.

I was very eager to go back to school. I missed my friends, I missed learning about science, and I even missed walking the five kilometers each morning and afternoon. I did not want to fall further behind than I already had, so I became very diligent about my schoolwork. I read further in the textbooks than the teachers required and turned assignments in on time. I joined Christian Union and stood before the students and recommitted my life to Christ. I offered to help make improvements to the library and went early to school carrying a borrowed hammer. I began to gain favor with the teachers and headmaster, and on the first day of school in my fourth and final year, they named me school captain.

The school fees continued to be a heavy burden. I saved up some of my newspaper commissions, bought a small camera, and started taking pictures. I developed the film as cheaply as I could and then sold the prints for a couple of shillings each. I took what I earned into the office of the headmaster every month and told him I wished for it to go toward school fees. It was not close to the amount I owed, but it was enough to show him I was trying. When it came time for the national examination, full payment to the government was mandatory. The headmaster saw there was no way I could pay. He paid for my registration fee using his own personal money. It is one of the most meaningful gifts I have ever received.

I passed the exams, officially graduated from secondary school, and was ready for my next step. I knew very well that God was calling me into ministry like my father. My heart, my mind, everything in me knew. My goal was to attend seminary in Nairobi, the dream city of every child in my village. But I would not be able to afford seminary, of course. There was only one in Nairobi, and it was a lot of money, but I thought there might be a way for me to go to the local Bible school. It was the lowest level of pastoral training, a two-year program, and it was cheap. I was very active in our local church, and when I expressed my interest to the elders about enrolling, they said they would be willing to send me.

The day I graduated from Bible school was the most proud I had ever seen my father. The graduation ceremony was conducted in Subukia village, and two lecturers from the seminary in Nairobi drove there to present us with our certificates. One was an American lecturer, and one a Kenyan. We knew they were coming, and to me they were like celebrities. When the ceremony was over, they said to all of the graduates, "Now that you are eligible to apply, keep our seminary in mind if you want to continue with your education."

That was my chance. That day was my day. Without a plan beyond a small suitcase, I approached the men and said, "If you don't mind, can you give me a lift?" They said yes and asked me where I was going. I told them I was going to seminary in Nairobi.

# CHAPTER THREE

# JUSTIN

We summited at night. Our guide, aptly named Teacher, woke us up at midnight, which was barely an hour after I managed to fall asleep, thanks to the howling wind and the sheet of ice that covered the tent in a blanket of cold. By midnight, the ice had grown so thick the porters had to chip it off so they could get my dad and me for our wake-up call. We bundled up in our jackets and beanies and trekking boots and headlamps and followed Teacher up the last stretch of Mount Kilimanjaro. At the time of our trek, Teacher had easily summited 250 times; by today, I'm sure he's surpassed his 600th climb. He wasn't wearing a headlamp. In fact, he had no light at all; he was simply in front of us, guiding in the pitch black.

The summit is always the hardest. It's that final stretch that separates the well prepared from the well intentioned. If a climber wasn't trained, if they hadn't developed their lung capacity, if they weren't acclimated, the summit was where they would fail. That night, as I trailed closely behind Teacher and my dad, I had a very real fear that this would happen to me. The trip was an expensive high school graduation gift from my dad; the thought of training for months, traveling all the way to Tanzania, and then getting altitude sickness and not making it to the top of my first climb was my worst nightmare.

The official altitude of the peak is 19,340 feet, which put our final seven-hour ascent right in the middle of an arctic zone. The terrain was mainly glacial silt, and it was hard to maneuver, even more so because of the gale-force winds, but the hardest part was the darkness. Our headlamps allowed us to see a few feet in front of us, but the black that surrounded us made it feel like we were walking into a great abyss. I had asked Teacher the day before why climbers summited at night, and he said, "If people could see what they were about to climb, they would not make it."

I can't say I enjoy the unknown. My dad and I did the trek more as a part of a plan to grow ourselves rather than in pursuit of the unknown. We are the type that take calculated risks and with proper preparation, measured routes, and reasonable expectations. We felt safe and qualified for the climb—my dad probably more than me, but I was used to following him into places that were beyond my comfort zone.

My mom had flown to Tanzania with us, and we went on safari for a few days prior to the climb, but then she flew back to be with my younger brother in Atlanta. I'm a born-and-raised Atlantan, born on the south side, in a suburb called Fayetteville, and raised in a Southern Baptist church. I like to tell people I was in church from the second I was born, if not nine months before. At four months old, I played the role of baby Jesus, with my mother as Mary, in a huge church production, and from there on out, we attended services every Sunday, come hell or high water. We also went on Wednesday nights for dinner in the fellowship hall, as any good Baptist does.

Our lives very much revolved around God and family. For most of my life, we lived within a fifteen-mile radius of the church, both sets of grandparents, and most of my uncles, aunts, and cousins. There was hardly a month we wouldn't get together to celebrate something or someone.

When I wasn't at church, I was at school. I started at a Montessori preschool about a year after my brother David was born. Some of my earliest memories revolve around learning. The Montessori school was a bright and colorful place where they believed early childhood education wasn't about filling kids with facts but about cultivating their natural desire to learn through playing. It worked. Through Legos and xylophones and puzzle maps and pin poking, I fell in love with learning and got a thrill from mastering new things. I learned enough Chinese at age four to string together a sentence, and for Christmas I asked Santa to bring me a dìqiú hé wàzi (a globe and socks).

"My work here is done," my dad said to my mom.

My brother didn't attend the Montessori school, although I really wanted him to; the idea of doing all of those activities together sounded like what brothers should be doing. At home, all David did was bite or scratch or hit me. Sometimes, he would make noises and scream, occasionally directed at me but most times directed at nothing and nobody. Those were the times we turned on the TV to find whichever channel was airing *Barney and Friends*. Somehow, that singing purple dinosaur always gave him peace.

When I wasn't at school or church, I was playing sports. I played baseball, football, golf, and soccer—anything with a ball—around our community, through different organizations, but I played basketball in the church league. That was in addition to being a Royal Ambassador, my church's equivalent to Boy Scouts. We met weekly, wore blue vests, and collected badges for feats like memorizing Bible verses, being pen pals with missionary kids, and participating in campouts, fitness challenges, derby races, and mission projects. I was dedicated to covering my vest with badges; I never did anything halfway.

When the badge called for knowing seventy-five memory verses, I went for eighty-five. When the middle school track coach challenged the team to run 200 miles over the summer, I woke up early each morning to get my run in even though I wasn't on the track team. When my math teacher said we could get extra credit if we memorized the first hundred digits of pi throughout the course of the school year, I gave myself the weekend to take what I knew—3.14—and commit the additional ninety-seven digits to memory.

I went into school the next Monday and announced, "I'd like to do the pi extra credit."

"All right, when?" she asked as she headed for the pledge calendar.

"Right now."

I stood up and did it. Bam—100 extra points.

My dad was always encouraging me to study, explore, and push myself to learn something I didn't know. We read countless books together and then discussed them. In middle school, I was reading Andy Stanley, John Ortberg, and John Maxwell. Sometimes we listened to audiotapes or attended conferences together, especially when my dad spoke at conferences and I was afforded the opportunity to tag along.

He traveled quite a bit, at least once a month, to speak either as part of his role at Chick-fil-A or on behalf of a ministry. I remember being ten years old and flying to Washington, DC, with him when he was helping train faith leaders in the Becoming a Contagious Christian curriculum, one of those classic '90s evangelism tools. One of the specifics in that curriculum was the bridge illustration, a drawing that offered a simple explanation of the Gospel. It depicted people on the left and God on the right, and because of sin, there was a chasm between the two. By drawing a cross, you created a bridge that signified how no one was stranded, unable to get back to the Creator.

My dad had me get up in front of what felt like a thousand people—realistically, probably 300 or 400—and I would take the audience through the illustration. As I stood there in my little suit and tie, I used an overhead projector to show the audience, step-by-step, how to draw it and how to communicate it to believers and nonbelievers alike. I assumed my dad had me do it to show the crowd that the bridge illustration was so easy that even a ten-year-old could do it. But afterward, he said to me, "Son, you belong in places that you may think are ahead of you, ahead of your time, or ahead of your age."

My mom and brother rarely accompanied my dad on his trips. I didn't always travel with him, but I definitely went more than both of them combined. The times my mom did come along meant my brother got to stay with my grandparents. There was one time I was jealous he was staying at Whitey and Bebe's house because I knew what a blast he would have. "He'll get to stay up late and eat oatmeal crème pies," I whined.

"Don't ever be envious of your brother!" my mom said, louder than her usual gentle demeanor. "He's never going to have all the opportunities you have."

That was one of the first and only times I recall it being pointed out to me that David had limitations. It was certainly the only time either parent made me feel guilty about it, and even then, it wasn't so much guilt as it was merely stating a fact.

When David was around six months old, my mom and dad noticed that David wasn't hitting some developmental milestones. He couldn't sit up, hadn't attempted to combat crawl across the kitchen floor, wasn't picking up on standard words like mama or dada, and wouldn't respond when someone tried to engage him—at least not in the way anyone expected him to respond.

Although my parents were never really given a firm diagnosis, the doctors said his symptoms most closely resembled cerebral palsy (CP) and autism. Unlike others with CP, it didn't affect David's muscles so much that he would be wheelchair bound; he was just extremely delayed in his physical and cognitive abilities. He learned to walk at three but never learned to communicate verbally.

David's limitations were our family's norm, and it never occurred to me to be bothered by his body splayed like a starfish on our living room floor when he had his spells of dizziness or the hectic energy he brought to our nightly routines. The music of Barney interjected with David's grunts and approving moans became the soundtrack of my life at home. There were times, though, when his differences were made clear to me by the way the outside world reacted to him.

One night, we went out for dinner after my parents had a particularly long week. The comfort and familiarity of Ted's Montana Grill was just what the doctor ordered that night, so we settled into our usual booth and ordered the classic round—a Coke for me, water for Mom, and sweet tea for Dad and David. David's drinks were always delivered in a covered Styrofoam cup. A plastic lid with the Sweet label popped inward assured my dad he was handing David the correct order, but the assurance was false. A cold bitter imitation of David's favorite drink awaited him in that Styrofoam cup. Our unassuming waitress had given David unsweet tea, a mistake that was unacceptable to his very particular palate.

Enraged by his first sip, David gripped the cup so tightly his fingers gouged right through the Styrofoam, like they had gouged into my mom's and dad's arms on occasion. Tea poured through the holes in the cup onto the table and across David's lap. Then, screaming, he launched the leaking cup across the Ted's dining room like a grenade. David's outbursts were always like launching a grenade.

The tables full of families and couples and businessmen all turned to us and stared. This wasn't a new occurrence; people tended to stare at him when we were in public, usually with kind eyes but staring all the same. David was never a source of embarrassment for me, and he wasn't that day either. David had the right to express himself how he could, just like anyone else, but seeing all those eyes on him did make me a little sad. As I watched him, covered in tea but drowning in the familiar pity that hung in the air, I was reminded that David would always be confined by an impenetrable stigma. He would always be placed inside a box or outside of one, depending on the observer. Those boxes would always define his place in society.

Another time, we were socializing in the church lobby after service, and David decided it was time to go. He did everything in his power to convince my dad to get up from his seat and get the family out the door, and for David, that didn't mean bargaining or reasoning with my dad like I sometimes did to get what I wanted; it meant an all-out physical brawl.

David started with the arms, hitting, scratching, slapping, but my dad had done this before, so he quickly restrained the hands. Without missing a beat, David moved to the legs, kicking, stomping, tripping. With his hands busy restraining David's arms, my dad fought foot with foot. While remaining seated and barely breaking concentration from his conversation, my dad used his legs to block David's kicks.

Dad had gotten good at playing defense. It looked as though David had been bested, but he never succumbed to reason or followed the plan. He wanted to go home, and there was no stopping him. With his hands and legs defeated, David used his head. With no warning, David headbutted my dad as hard as he could. It worked. David immediately had my dad's full attention (and everyone else's).

But my dad wasn't mad. He winced in pain for a split second and then immediately looked up and smiled. My dad's emotions lived between optimistic and enthusiastic. He never cried, he never yelled, and, especially in situations regarding David, he always stuck to the plan. It was moments like this when I realized how much like my dad I really was. Well-made plans and well-charted paths gave me comfort and held me together.

I'm sure it was very hard to be the parents of someone with extreme special needs, but I wouldn't know because they never said so. My mom, who arguably carried the heaviest load as the primary caregiver, didn't seem fazed by it. She left her job as a computer programmer at Delta Air Lines to stay home with me and David, but I don't think she expected to spend the next thirty years caring for an eternal toddler. She exuded joy over caring for David and never spoke about the sacrifices she made because I don't think she believes she made any.

Both she and my dad went about their daily routines, treating us as any loving parents would treat their sons. They inspected both of our mouths to make sure our teeth were brushed properly, even though they were the ones who brushed David's teeth. They took us to Zoo Atlanta and bought both of us safari hats to wear on the endangered species carousel, even though David never went on it. They bought a trampoline for the backyard that they made clear was for us to share, although David mostly lay in the middle of it while I jumped around him. The first thing my dad would do when he got home each night was take off whichever Chick-fil-A tie he'd worn that day, drape his suit jacket over a chair, and ask if anybody wanted to go outside to play Ultimate Frisbee. David never took him up on the offer, but I said yes enough for both of us.

Ultimate Frisbee, or just Ultimate as the devotees call it, was big in our house. Disc golf too. In fact, every time my dad and I traveled together, we put two or three discs in our suitcase and tracked down a disc golf course. It didn't matter where in the country we went; we found a way to play.

It was not only a fun physical activity, but it also gave us intentional time to connect. We had hundreds if not thousands of conversations while throwing discs. We talked about school, books, girls, church, sports, and life in general. Nothing was off-limits. It was during one of those talks that my dad proposed we build on our habit of learning things we didn't know and start doing things we'd never done. If reading books expanded our minds, experiences would surely expand our understanding. We agreed to do one new thing every year that stretched us. New experiences were now part of our well-laid plans.

During summers, I attended Camp WinShape in Rome (the city in northwest Georgia, not the other one). We weren't a big camping family, but I loved being outside, building forts, and exploring the woods with my friends, so Camp WinShape gave me an ideal outlet. They had so many sessions campers could take—archery, basketball, rock climbing, horseback riding, rappelling, soccer—and they used a system of nine ranks in which advancement hinged on showing good character. Campers who put in enough years rising through the ranks were eligible to take the infamous Little Chief test, a grueling eighteen-hour feat of exertion that required different physical and mental skills. Passing it was the highest rank awarded to a camper; it was what everyone dreamed about. Especially me.

I was thirteen years old the year I was finally selected to compete. If I passed, I would be the youngest person to ever become a Little Chief. They woke up about twenty campers at midnight and took us to the dining hall, where they read a charge explaining the various elements of the test and then put a speaking ban on us. From that point forward, one sound or word from any candidate meant elimination. They took us outside and told us to build a fire with only one match and some firewood; we couldn't use sticks or leaves or pine cones. We had to keep the fire going for six hours. A handful of boys couldn't do it and were eliminated, but not me. I made it to the next round.

The second round required that we run a mile and a half straight up the side of a mountain. There were pacers who ran next to us, and we had to keep up; if a candidate passed the pacer in the front or was passed by the pacer in the back, the candidate failed the test. Of course, the pacers were swapped out at three different points along the run, so they had fresh legs, which made our exhaustion all the more evident. Out of all the Little Chief test rounds, most people who failed did so during the run, and that's exactly what happened to me. I failed without even making it to the second leg of the run. It was devastating, and I felt sorry for myself for about two minutes, until I channeled my dad and tried to handle it with his positive outlook. There was no need for me to be devastated when I could be determined instead.

I got selected to take the test again the following year, and what made my second chance even more exciting was that my best friend Josh was selected too. Josh and I met in fourth grade, when I transferred from the Montessori school to a private Christian school. All the students were required to choose an elective, and Josh and I found ourselves sitting next to each other when we both chose band. The other students had already called dibs on all the instruments except for the trombone. Of course, that was the one assigned to me. Josh had signed up to play saxophone, but his parents made him switch after they were randomly given a hand-me-down trombone. Nothing bonds people quite like being the only two trombone players in band class.

Four years later, we were together at WinShape and thrilled about the possibility of becoming Little Chiefs together. Our parents were at home, desperately praying we'd both make it; if one of us did and one of us didn't, they knew it would be too hard for the loser to swallow. The night finally came, and we were taken to the dining hall at midnight, where the speaking ban was enforced. We walked outside to begin building our fires, and it started to rain. It didn't just sprinkle; it poured. Out of the twenty-four boys taking the test, only four survived that first challenge. Josh and I were two of them.

Next was the mountain run. I tried to play it as safe as I could by keeping consistent speed in between the front and back pacers. I became so focused that I didn't notice whether Josh was still running or how muddy the ground had become—or that I had completed the second leg. Only three survived that second challenge, and Josh and I were two of them.

The next challenge was to write a 1,500-word essay about what Camp WinShape meant to us. Luckily for both of us, the essay was judged on length, not on eloquence. In fact, Josh later told me that he wrote about how a certain passage of Scripture applied to his experience at Camp WinShape and then proceeded to copy an entire chapter of the Bible into the essay. The third guy in our final trio wrote nothing. Only two survived that third challenge: Josh and me.

That left the last segment of manual labor, where we helped set up for the final ceremony of camp by lifting logs, shoveling dirt, and pulling weeds. It was tedious, but at that point, it felt like smooth sailing. Josh and I were exhausted, starving, and filthy, but the hardest part was not speaking to each other about how excited we were to be the only two out of the entire group to make it through the test.

At the final Council Ring ceremony, we were given the official rank of Little Chief, along with a breastplate made of beads, an eagle feather, and a knife engraved with our newly bestowed Little Chief name: Josh's was Confident Catamount, and mine was Noble Griffin. All the parents came to that final day of camp and attended the ceremony. I beamed with pride when I spotted my parents in the crowd. I could tell my mom and dad were excited for me, although they were probably more relieved than anything else, since they'd had to endure my year of running up every hill I could find and my insistence on starting every fire we made in our fireplace.

After that summer, David started at a new school for kids with special needs and got really into Sesame Street. I started ninth grade at my private school and got really into basketball. I think I played too many sports as a kid to ever master any one of them, which, in my drive for perfection, was more aggravating than I cared to admit. When I was called up to the varsity basketball team during my freshman year, I took that as a sign to go all in. I played for the next four years and thrived, not necessarily because I was a great athlete but because I had a great coach. At times, it felt like Coach B thought he was coaching a Division I college program—mandatory practice on Christmas Day, national tournaments from Durham to Delaware, running drills that impressed even the stars of our track team, year-round conditioning—but his passion and commitment to the players and the game were contagious. He helped to develop in me a grit and discipline that hadn't been there before, and it influenced how hard I worked academically too.

"Nothing worth having ever comes easy" was written on a piece of paper inside of my locker. Next to it was a note from my dad that said, Colossians 3:23: "Whatever you do, work at it with all your heart as working for the Lord and not for man."

I was committed to attending a good college and, in my typical overachiever fashion, set my sights on getting into an Ivy League. I was shaping up to be the valedictorian of my graduating class and had solid test scores, so I felt relatively confident when I applied to Princeton, Yale, and Columbia. And even though they weren't Ivy League, I also applied to Duke, Stanford, Vanderbilt, and Georgia Tech, although the idea of staying in my hometown for college felt way too safe.

Despite my full plate of basketball, study groups, student council, and church, my dad and I kept up our yearly tradition of doing something that stretched us. We went rafting on the Snake River in Idaho, deep-sea fishing in Florida, and did a basketball exchange program in China, which doubled as a mission trip with our church. I also went on short-term mission trips to places like Birmingham, Puerto Rico, and Honduras. My parents had always impressed on me the importance of giving back, but it wasn't until I went on those trips that I realized they also meant through my presence and compassion. Those were things I could give away for free and that meant just as much—or, in some cases, more—to the receiver.

My week in Honduras was during spring break of my senior year, and I flew home on a high after a great trip. I was quickly brought back to earth when I saw a stack of college admission responses waiting for me. All but one of the envelopes were too thin. In that moment, I dropped any feeling of satisfaction or joy I had gathered in the preceding week in Honduras. Everything came down to what school I got into. If I didn't get into the right school, I wasn't going to get anything right after that. I put in all that work so I could go to the best college, get into the best grad school, land the best job, make the best living, and live the best life. That was the plan.

I didn't get into Princeton, Yale, Columbia, Duke, or Stanford. I got accepted into Georgia Tech, and I had been waitlisted at Vanderbilt. Getting rejected by the schools I held in such esteem was a shock to my system. From as early as I could remember, those things defined me—a high grade point average, accolades on my resume, starting position on varsity, church involvement, community volunteer hours; now, they no longer could. Acceptance into an Ivy League college was where I placed my worth. What would become of me now that I failed? I graduated as the valedictorian and addressed the student body with no clue as to where I was going to go to school.

Weeks later, I was trekking Mount Kilimanjaro with my dad.

There was a lot of downtime in camp at the end of each day, so he and I read a book together—*The Barbarian Way* by Erwin McManus. We took turns reading aloud, and as we got further into the chapters, the message of the book began to resonate with me. McManus wasn't raised in a Christian home and didn't come to know Christ until college. His journey from there—including his relationship with God and view of the church—was unconventional. McManus's heart for God was untamed, and he encouraged believers to acknowledge that Christ never promised a proper or safe religion, and He certainly never promised an easy road that was precisely mapped out. Instead, He beckoned His followers to a path filled with adventure, uncertainty, and unlimited possibilities. The book called for readers to escape "civilized" Christianity and embrace whatever path God sent them down, no matter the cost.

We finished reading the book the same night we successfully summited. That night, in the freezing darkness, as we battled our way toward the top of the peak, I knew I was on the right path. I couldn't see—only enough to take the next few steps—and I had absolutely no idea what lay ahead, but I knew I needed to trust the guide. I knew I needed to walk forward and brace myself for adventure, uncertainty, and unlimited possibilities.

# CHAPTER FOUR

# DUNCAN

It was a long drive from Subukia to Nairobi, which meant I had at least three hours to think about what I had just done. I did not know how I would get into seminary school once we arrived, and I did not know what I would say to the lecturers if they asked any questions. At that moment, I did not have any answers. I told them I was not feeling well and needed to rest. That was not the truth, but I did not want to risk ruining my chance with conversation. I needed time to sort out what I planned to do once I arrived. All I knew was that I was going to Nairobi, the place I had dreamed about my whole life, the capital city. My imagination told me to get ready for tall buildings, job opportunities, paved roads, and running water.

I listened to the lecturers talk while I pretended to be asleep in the back seat. I overheard them speaking about seminary and the parts of the syllabus they still needed to cover before the end of the term. I listened to them discussing the students and the promise they showed during their sermon preparation during the homiletics course. I took notes in my mind when they talked about staff housing and the new lecture hall being built on the grounds of Brackenhurst. Maybe that was the name of the school? Brackenhurst, I repeated to myself over and over. All that was happening was confusing and exciting, and I went from curious to nervous to grateful to shy to sorry to brave and back again. I felt so much all at once that I could not say what I felt most.

When the car slowed down, I knew we must have been getting closer to Nairobi. I sat up slowly, to make it look natural, opened my eyes slowly, and looked out the window to see the city for the very first time. Another three hours of imagining could not have prepared me for what I saw. Even though it was night, practically ten o'clock by then, it almost seemed like daytime because of all the lights. Streetlights, traffic lights, porch lights, headlights, and brake lights were shining from every direction. I had never seen that many before. Only once before had I witnessed electricity in Nakuru. I had seen some lights from public transportation vehicles, but never vehicles and streets and buildings at the same time. It felt even greater and more important than I had expected, and it caused the knot in my stomach to twist and turn.

"So where in Nairobi are you staying? Where should we drop you off?" the American asked.

"Brackenhurst," I repeated out loud this time, using my new information and hoping that was indeed the place of seminary.

"Oh, that is good. That is where we are going too," the Kenyan said.

I said nothing else, and neither did they. God helped them not to ask me more questions.

I kept my focus on the window and saw a side road with a big metal sign that went from one light post to another. Brackenhurst, it read. The road was narrow, just enough for two cars to pass each other going opposite ways, and it began to incline immediately. It curved often, and I realized we were driving up the side of a mountain. The beam of the headlights showed a lot of trees on either side of the paved path, like we were driving through a forest. Were we? Up and up we went until we reached a large gate next to a guardhouse. The guards saw that the car held faculty members and waved us right through. I could not believe my luck.

The first thing I noticed inside the gate was a bunch of white children running around on a large grass area, with big lights shining down on them. I do not know what surprised me more, seeing white people or seeing green grass in the middle of the dry season. The lecturers did not seem surprised, and they kept driving past what looked like little homes, although they were bigger than my family's home in the village. I saw walking paths lined with lampposts and a lot of trees and lanterns. There were also larger structures that seemed more formal. Were they restaurants? Or classrooms? Assembly halls? There was so much to take in. It was like a hidden world within the city. I had never seen anything like it.

The two men asked where they should let me out, and I told them, "Just drop me at reception, please. I will be fine from there." I did not even know whether Brackenhurst had a reception. I closed my eyes and said a quick prayer.

When I opened them again, we were approaching a small building with big wooden doors that had the word "Welcome" carved across them as if they were expecting me. I thanked the men for giving me a ride and walked inside to find the lights turned down and the front desk empty. I sat down in one of the chairs that lined the wall and waited. I figured someone would come out soon. No one would leave doors unlocked in a place this nice. But when I sat alone for an hour and still no one came, I walked back outside to see what I could find.

Despite the late hour, there were still people walking around. I began to explore and realized that Brackenhurst was far larger than I ever would have thought. It was not a seminary. It was a compound that housed a seminary. Later, I would learn that the hundred-acre land was purchased by the Baptist Mission of Kenya in the 1960s and transformed from a farm, hotel, and golf course into a divinity school, missionary housing, and church conference site.

Then, finally, I saw some Kenyan students on the grass field. At least I assumed they were students because they wore backpacks. They looked to be my age, and I watched as they walked from one side of the grass to the other and then onto a path headed away from me. I followed them as they went up a small hill and passed a dining hall, what looked to be some classrooms, and then the dormitories.

I headed straight for the entrance of the dormitories the moment I saw it. Lodging! I entered a large room of bunk beds and was surprised to see that not all of the beds were taken. I went to the corner where there was a free bed on a bottom bunk, put my stuff down, and relaxed a little, knowing that at least I had found myself a bed for the night.

I survived in seminary for two months. No one questioned my sudden appearance, because both the students and teachers thought I was a new student. I walked with the students into the dining hall, and the servers did not say anything. I attended lectures, and the teachers noticed me, but they did not stop me. Through will and false confidence, I became one of them. I became a seminary student in Nairobi. It was a miracle. My two months came to an end with the end of the school year. As it did, I prayed and asked God to open a way for me to stay.

I was hanging around the reception area when the wife of the seminary music teacher recognized me and asked what classes I was planning to enroll in.

"I am not sure. I am looking into options," I told her.

"You are from Nakuru. Is that right?" she asked in her American accent.

I did not know how she knew, but I nodded and said yes.

"My husband and I have started a gap year program for young people who want to go into ministry. It's an opportunity to serve in East Africa for one year before starting college. The Baptist Mission is sponsoring the program, and we're looking for eight students from across the country. We don't have anybody from Nakuru yet. Would you like to be a candidate?"

I nodded harder and said yes louder than before. She handed me some papers to fill out and told me that the auditions were being held the next day. The program was called IMPACT, which stood for International Mission Performing Arts Christian Team. Along with door-to-door evangelism, the program used drama and music as a way to share the Gospel with others. She asked if I had done anything like that before. This time, I nodded gently without saying yes, which made it feel like less of a lie. I auditioned the next day with other students. We sang together and read the script they gave us. A week later, I found out I had been accepted.

The group of students who were chosen had five boys and three ladies, and they gave us two small homes at Brackenhurst, one for the boys and one for the girls, to live in while we trained. Since I was already living in the compound, I was the first to arrive at the boys' home. I let myself in and found a main living area, a small kitchen, one bathroom, and three bedrooms. Two of the bedrooms had bunk beds that were to be shared, and the third room had a single bed. I put my suitcase onto the single bed and waited for the others to arrive. By nightfall, three of the other boys had joined me, and we were only waiting on the last one. His name was Cornel, and I was told he was the leader. One of the other boys said Cornel had done the program the year before and had been asked to return to oversee the new team. But I did not wait to meet him. I went to sleep before he got there so I would be rested for the new start.

I met Cornel early the next morning as I came out of my bedroom. We introduced ourselves and shook hands, and then the five of us boys went to the dining hall for breakfast before our first day of training.

"Duncan," Cornel said when we returned to the home, "would you like to move to the other room now?"

"Why? I am comfortable in this room."

"I think it would be better if you shared with one of the teammates."

I thanked him for the suggestion and insisted that I was fine in my room. He looked at me for a moment longer, without saying anything, before he smiled.

"All right. That is good then," he said finally before he walked away.

From January through March, we trained at Brackenhurst. We practiced songs, memorized our roles in short parable plays, studied Bible passages, learned how to share our testimonies, and reviewed the ways people might react as we went door to door. Cornel kept our schedule, made sure we were prepared for each specific training, and assigned us our weekly duties. He always gave us meeting times that were earlier than the time we needed to be there, he triple-checked that we had our notebooks or Bibles or hymnals, and he seemed to make sure each of us was assigned the chore we hated most. Maybe I should have told him how I was in charge of my whole secondary school when I was school captain, to show him I didn't need his guidance.

In April, after three months of training, our group of eight began our work. We got in a van and left to minister throughout Kenya, Uganda, and Tanzania. We would be traveling for the next nine months, and despite being strangers only weeks before, we had all become good friends. Only Cornel and I seemed to have some distance still between us. We were guarded around each other, or maybe the better word is sensitive. I assumed it was because he was a Luo and I was a Kikuyu. We knew it from the moment we met. We could see it in each other's faces and hear it in our accents. I do not believe there was any hate between us, but we knew our opposing tribes had endured decades of conflict, most of which were political, and we had been raised to not trust each other. Genuinely liking each other, or even simply getting along, went against our nature.

The experiences of our team over the next few months were filled with great range. We traveled through urban and rural areas, staying with host families who lived in formal homes and slums. Some days we ate well, and others we hardly ate at all. We spoke at crusades and to individuals on the street, witnessed at large hospitals and run-down clinics, felt welcomed and avoided. During such a demanding season, we relied on each other for support, energy, confidence, and guidance. Cornel was always the first to offer it.

As we went from village to village, there were times when the American founder of the program, Cindy, was with us and became the leader over Cornel. One of the times she joined us was in Tanzania, when we went to minister to a local church. We all walked into the sanctuary together and immediately stopped, stunned. An entire congregation stood before us, screaming, falling down, dancing, and casting out demons. It was theatrics like we had never seen and felt very extreme. We were not used to that in our Kenyan culture, and even for our American, it was too much. Cindy took us outside and told us we should go back to Kenya and cancel that mission.

"May I kindly encourage you to reconsider?" Cornel asked. "It is an uncomfortable scene in there, but perhaps you are making an emotional decision."

I could tell he felt uneasy saying that to the leader, especially because she was a lady. It could be viewed as disrespectful to challenge a female in authority, so for him to say anything meant he must have felt very firm in his belief that we stay.

"No, I think we should go back. I don't think they'll hear us over their antics," she said.

"I think we should find a way to still do the mission," Cornel said gently. "We do not need to stay at this church, but we felt God was calling us to Tanzania for a reason."

The other members of the team agreed with Cindy that it was best to leave.

"If you go, I kindly ask to stay behind and complete what I feel we are supposed to do," Cornel said, with his hands together as if in prayer.

Cindy and the others looked hesitant so Cornel tried one more time.

"What they are doing inside that church is not biblical. Is there a way we can help instead of running away?"

I not only agreed with Cornel, but I was also proud of his conviction.

"I agree with Cornel on this," I said.

Cornel looked surprised, and I knew why. In the six months we had known each other, he was used to me being the one to challenge him, not to agree with him.

The group ended up staying in Tanzania to continue our ministry. That night, we went to a hostel just outside Tabora, but their vacancy was limited. They only had a few open beds, which meant the eight students needed to share, with one single bed left for Cindy.

"No, the single bed should go to Cornel," Cindy said. "Much like it is in the Brackenhurst house, the team leader is the one to have their own space."

I froze. The single room in which I slept had been meant for Cornel because he was the leader. Cornel must have noticed the realization on my face because he put his hand on my shoulder and whispered, "It was no trouble, my friend."

That was the beginning of our friendship. Yes, when I look back on my relationship with Cornel, I see it was in Tanzania that the shift took place. We slowly began to feel more comfortable around each other and started to talk about things other than the missions. We spoke of our families and our villages, his struggles with school and mine with health. I told him the story of how I ended up at Brackenhurst and confided that I had never seen a toilet before, so on my first night I used its water to brush my teeth and wash my face. He told me he received a flier about the IMPACT ministry program at his secondary school because a Baptist church sponsored them. His father was not happy about his decision to leave for Nairobi. I started to really respect Cornel, both as a leader and as a brother, and I sensed that he began to respect me as well.

The two of us had a conversation in Tanzania about what we were going to do after the program ended, although we still had about three more months to go. I shared with him my deep desire to attend seminary, and he said he was probably going to head back to his village to find work and help support his family. I was surprised to hear he was not thinking about seminary. I thought he would be a very good candidate, and I told him so.

"I do not think I am called to be a pastor," Cornel said. "And there is not a way for me to pay for seminary, even if I wished to go."

"There are many reasons people attend seminary, not just to become a pastor. And yes, money is a problem for me also. I have to believe that God will provide."

And then He did.

When we returned to Brackenhurst, Cindy and her husband, Keith, asked all eight of us what we planned to do now that IMPACT was ending. By that time, Cornel felt that seminary was indeed where he was meant to be. He said that God used me to guide his path in that direction. So both Cornel and I told them of our intentions, and they asked to speak with us privately later that afternoon. As the four of us walked along the paths of Brackenhurst, they told us that they felt they knew us well by then. They knew our hearts and knew there was much good that God wanted to do through us.

"We have a friend who wants to help you both," Cindy said. That is when she introduced us to Lynn Burrow. Lynn was on the ministry team with Cindy and wanted to personally see to it that Cornel and I attend seminary.

"I will pay your school fees," Lynn said. "And the only thing I ask in return is that you join us for mission work during some of your breaks."

I would not consider Cornel or myself to be emotional, but during that conversation, we were both visibly moved. Neither of us knew what to say, which was especially uncommon for me. We embraced Lynn and Cindy and Keith and whispered thank you over and over again. They enrolled us that very day for the upcoming school year, and it would have been hard to find two people more grateful or excited. Cornel and I had already planned on leaving Brackenhurst to see our families for Christmastime, but now we had a reason to return.

My mother and father were very happy to see me. I had written telling them of my visit, but letters were not always delivered reliably, so they did not know to expect me. When I arrived, they slaughtered one of our goats and gathered my siblings, aunt and uncle, and neighbors together for a special meal to hear about the year that had gone by. They were interested in my travels and very pleased to hear about my enrollment in seminary. I shared with them about Cornel, how he was on the team of people I ministered with, and how he was also going to be joining me at school.

My father asked where he was from, and I told him Kisumu. It took me several seconds to realize how quiet it had become.

"He is a Luo?" my father asked. His tone was not as alarmed as his eyes.

"He is," I said casually.

"Duncan, be careful. Those people, that tribe, we do not trust them."

"I know that is how it has been in the past."

"Luo do not get circumcised."

To my father, that was probably worse than anything else. Circumcision was a ritual practice in our culture that marked the passage from boyhood to manhood. It was an anticipated and honorable event in which males of fourteen or fifteen years of age were taken down to the river to face the knife bravely without flinching. Any sign of pain or fear brings shame to them and their family, although not nearly as much as being uncircumcised. My father strongly believed that circumcision was biblical and that males who did it were more mature and had wisdom in matters of life. I was now friends with someone who was uncircumcised, and that alone was worthy of disgrace.

"There are other tribes that do not perform circumcision, not just Luo," I said.

"And we do not associate with them either," my father said.

It was an old way of thinking. It reminded me of the hushed conversations I listened in on during my months of sickness. How my father talked about the man who died of AIDS. I had learned a lot during my year of ministry and felt I had grown in the areas of tolerance and acceptance. That was not only because of my interactions with different cultures and communities or my friendship with someone in a rival tribe but also because of the education I received from the Baptist Mission. Before we left for our missions, we were counseled on how to approach people in relational and loving ways. Lead with love, they told us. They taught us about the diseases we would see as we traveled, like diphtheria, yellow fever, and HIV/AIDS, and they corrected common misunderstandings of those illnesses so that our minds were not narrow and we would not react poorly to those who suffered.

I do not believe the members of my family intended to be unchristianlike. They only believed what they knew to be true. I left my village wondering if minds could ever truly be changed.

Cornel and I returned to Brackenhurst for seminary that January. Unlike last time, I was officially a student and selected music as my major. Cornel elected theology. We had three school breaks a year, each one a month long, and we did as we promised and ministered around East Africa with Cindy and Keith. It was nice to use what we learned in our classes to better preach the Word. We liked that we were able to grow in our skills while doing important work. Most of the time, our interactions with people made us feel lighter, like lifting others up lifted us up too.

It was in our second year of seminary that we returned to Tanzania on our own, only Cornel and me. We were in a small village on the outskirts of Dodoma, going door to door just as we had many times before, but that time it felt different. Heavier. It was not just the increase of negative reactions from people, although that was noticeably higher. It was the sorrow in the voices who sent us away. Door after door, we were met with despair and anger.

"Jesus is not our priority!"

"Why would we follow a God that cannot even deliver us from this suffering?"

One woman physically kicked us out of her home while she screamed, "I will not praise a God who killed my son!"

We had seen enough black Xs painted above boarded doors to know that it had only taken a few years for AIDS to devastate the community. Large numbers of people had died or been forced to leave, and the few who remained were forced to bear the burden of what little was left behind. Those who had the disease fought for their lives without help or understanding. And those who were not infected still suffered because the community was labeled unclean. Their neighbors intentionally avoided their markets, and their livelihoods were reduced to nothing. Could we expect them to give their attention to Jesus when their most basic needs went unmet?

Cornel and I felt defeated. It was hard to see people in such pain and so sad that they were not able to hear how God could be their comfort. Still, we wandered through the village and prayed for those we passed. At the height of the afternoon sun, we saw a large baobab tree in the middle of a small field. It cast a shadow big enough for us to stretch out below it and find an escape from the heat that now felt more like fire.

"What was a problem before has turned into complete devastation," I said as I sat down and placed my Bible beside me.

Cornel was silent, the kind of silent that meant he was deep in thought.

"This reminds me of my village," he said finally.

"The disease or the despair?" I asked.

"Both. And the black Xs."

I lay down flat while Cornel sat cross-legged and slowly pulled at blades of brown grass.

"It has gotten far worse," he said. "The last few times I have gone home, I have seen it. Homes are abandoned. Children are alone in the streets. Some are with old grandparents. Some are living in orphanages. There is so much death. Those who are not dead are dying. Those who are not dying are only judging those who are."

I thought about my own village. If people had AIDS, they were suffering in silence either because they were trying to hide it or because they had no one to speak about it with. They were bound by shame and the fear of discrimination. They could not even find acceptance in church, which I knew because I had seen it with my own eyes.

"I am tired of these kinds of deaths, Duncan. Something needs to be done." Cornel took a deep breath and said, "I feel that my calling is to care for these people living with HIV/AIDS."

I rose to my elbows first and then slowly sat up to face him. "I have not heard this from you before," I told him. I thought of the many things we had discussed over the years, which even included AIDS when it was relevant to mission work, and Cornel had not mentioned an interest of this depth.

"It has been burning in my heart," he said. "I feel like I need to do something, but I do not know what or how."

I recalled a memory from long before, when I was very ill during secondary and heard my father as he met with women from the church about a funeral for someone with AIDS. I wondered what happened to that man who died. Did he ever receive a proper burial? Were those who knew him able to honor his life? Were they given a chance to love him despite the way he died?

"Somebody needs to speak about this in more than a small, tiny room," I said to Cornel as much as to myself. There was a breeze then. It was about half a minute of cool air that cut through the heat and filled us with relief. Afterward, stillness. Not the absence of air as much as the presence of peace.

"This is the ministry that God has been calling us to do," one of us said, although I do not recall which one. All I recall was that that moment felt holy. Under the tree, sitting next to my best friend, we felt that God had spoken clearly to us, more than any other time before or since.

Cornel and I went into our third year of seminary with clear direction. I think we were the only two in our whole college who did not plan on going somewhere to be a pastor after graduation.

As we worked hard toward finishing our degree, we still spent much of our school breaks evangelizing with Lynn and Cindy and Keith. We were also given the opportunity to volunteer as tour guides and translators for missionary groups hosted by the Baptist Mission.

The summer before our final year, a group of Americans came from Virginia Beach, and we were blessed to be their guides. They were a larger team so we split them into four groups. I was in charge of a group of three, and together, we moved from one slum house to another to share the Gospel. In Huruma, we saw a small church wedged between a shack that sold cabbages and a pharmacy that had long been forgotten. To get to the church, we hopped across the shallow ditch filled with sewage that lined the side of the dusty dirt road. Children had been following us, which was typical when they saw white people in any slum, but they scattered as we entered the church. There was a boy inside, though. He was small, maybe around five years, and was cleaning the pews with a cloth. One of the women in my group, known as Laura, asked me, "Duncan, who's that boy?"

"I do not know," I told her.

"Duncan, you should know that boy. You live here."

"I do not live in this village. I am a Kenyan, but I do not live in this spot, so how would I know that one boy from another?"

Laura went over and crouched down so she was eye to eye with him and then reached into her bag and gave him a candy bar.

"I am in love with that little boy," she told me as we left.

Day one, day two, day five, every day we did ministry in that slum, Laura saw the child. He followed us much of the time, and I told her it was because he was looking for more candy bars. As we left the slum on the final day of her trip, she held me very tight and began to cry.

"Duncan, can I take the boy home?"

"Sure, why not? Take him plus more boys."

She was not pleased with my joke. "You don't get it," she said. "I must help that boy."

"There are hundreds of children here, and I do not know their families, but I know they belong here. They all have somebody. They are good here." I did not know if that was true, but I did not know what to do with her emotions. There was nothing she could do to help him anyway.

That was Friday. On Wednesday of the following week, in the middle of the night, something woke me up. I could not go back to sleep, because there was a voice inside my head that would not be silent.

Duncan, you should know that boy.

Instantly, I was robbed of any peace I had felt. I had seen a boy in need, right in front of me, and I had turned my face. Instead, it was an American, who lived thousands of miles away, who clearly saw his longing. Was I too used to seeing people in need? Had I become numb to it? What had she seen that I had missed? What was so special about that little boy? I was overcome with emotions, just as Laura had been, and I started to sob. I lay awake, plagued by questions, until the moment I saw the light of the sun. Then I got dressed and walked eighteen kilometers back to the Huruma slum.

This time, there were no white people around so the boy did not show up. When I walked around for a while and did not see him, I went back home. I returned the next day and the day after until it became my job for the next two weeks. Every day I went to the slum, and every day I went back home feeling disappointed. Until one day, I found him. I saw him and knew right away that it was the same boy.

I knelt down to his level just as Laura had. "What is your name?"

"George," he said softly.

"Where are your parents?"

He could not explain himself beyond his name. Growing up in a slum can slow your growth and speech and everything else. I asked some adults and was told that his parents used to live there, but his father had died several years earlier, and the mother had been buried recently. He had siblings, but they were scattered throughout the slums. I asked who he lived with, and they said the whole community. He just showed up to a home and slept there, woke up in the morning, scavenged for food, and found another place to sleep the next night once it got dark.

I could not leave him. I knew it in my heart. I asked both the chief of the area and the pastor of Huruma Baptist Church if I could take George home with me. They gave me the same response I gave the American. "Yes, you can take him, and you can take all the other orphans here too."

I took George home with me, and from that day forward, he was my son.

# CHAPTER FIVE

# JUSTIN

By the time I was officially accepted into Vanderbilt, they had run out of freshman dorm space. The process of moving off the waitlist was more labor intensive than I had anticipated, and I called in every favor I had available—additional recommendation letters, calls to the provost, a prominent alum lobbying on my behalf. When I was offered my official acceptance, it came with the caveat that the school was willing to take a chance on me because of the outpouring of support. I was relieved not to be in limbo anymore, but to be honest, the victory was slightly soured knowing that my personal striving alone was not enough to get me in. After years of meticulous effort, it was my community that granted me success, not my sheer force of will.

I certainly was ready for a new chapter of life, but that chapter wouldn't start at the freshman dorms as I had always imagined. It would start in an upperclassmen residence hall, where school administrators converted tiny closets into what they hoped would pass as dorm rooms.

"It's cozy!" my parents said in unison when we walked into the room the day they moved me in.

It wasn't how I had envisioned my first year as a college student. While most freshmen were getting acclimated in close proximity to each other, a handful of other waitlisters turned students and I lived practically off campus. I knew early on that I'd have to be very intentional about putting myself out there if I wanted to meet people, although being assertive in social situations was not my norm.

One night, I went for it. I walked from the outskirts of campus to one of the freshman dorms. I hung around the lobby like I belonged there and ended up meeting a guy named John, who told me about a Bible study he'd started with other freshman guys. He invited me to go, and the next week, I did. I showed up to his dorm room—which was at least three times bigger than mine—and met a group of Christian guys who quickly welcomed me into their circle of friends. What were the odds of that happening all at once? It felt like I had met the right people at the right time, and everything had clicked into place. It finally felt like I was a student at Vanderbilt for a reason. The insecurities I carried about the circumstances of my school acceptance fell away as I settled into my life on campus.

During that first year at Vanderbilt, I joined the Beta Upsilon Chi fraternity along with most of the guys in my Bible study. I declared economics as my major, joined the Ultimate team, got involved with Campus Crusade for Christ, and was offered an internship over the summer with a youth leadership program called Student Leadership University. It was a fulfilling year, and I looked forward to telling Josh, my WinShape Little Chief comrade, all about it.

Josh went to Liberty University, in Virginia, after we graduated from high school. We stayed in touch as well as we could in our pre-smartphone world. Josh even registered me for a Facebook account (I was a late adopter) so we could keep up with each other's college escapades. We saw each other over Christmas break and agreed to plan a road trip over the summer to properly catch up. After I was offered the internship, one week of which had me traveling to California, we decided to make it a cross-country adventure and to go all the way to the West Coast. From there, we'd drive northeast to Illinois so I could meet up with my dad for the Global Leadership Summit.

The summit was an annual conference my dad had attended for as long as I could remember. It was a two-day event in South Barrington, right outside of Chicago, at Willow Creek Church. I had gone for the first time the year before, although it wasn't intended to be a conference for young people. When it started back in the mid-1990s, it was developed specifically to help pastors bring leadership best practices into church culture. Over the years, it morphed into being relevant to a group of people that was much broader, from marketplace leaders to philanthropists to academics. Although I wasn't any of those things, there was a lot to be gained by attending alongside my dad. I was used to being the youngest person in the room, and by the time I was in college, I understood the value of those experiences. This particular year, though, I was thrilled to have an accomplice. Zach was coming with me.

My friendship with Zach started casually. He would admit now that he was reluctant to hang out with me because I was a bit of a straitlaced nerd at the time. We met after my dad and his dad started a small biweekly men's leadership group, and our families began to see each other regularly. Zach went to a public school for the first part of his education, but he became my classmate in a private Christian school sophomore year. His dad had hoped that proximity to other Christians might ignite his passion for faith.

If I was the straitlaced guy who followed all the rules, Zach was the guy who tied those laces together so I would trip over them. He was never mean-spirited, just mischievous. It was immediately clear that Zach was a natural born leader. He had a presence that won him friends and admirers who were ready to join in his hijinks, and that included me. From skipping class to the occasional friendly house egging, he was always coming up with ideas that got us into trouble. Looking back, I'm glad I followed Zach into trouble. It was an opportunity for me to learn some important life lessons and, in the end, made me more resolute in my identity as a rule follower.

We had a small high school—about ninety people in each grade—so everyone wound up being friends with everyone. Even so, Josh remained my constant. He was the friend who was at the dinner table with my family even when I was at a late basketball practice and who had an overnight bag permanently packed and waiting in his car just in case I called. Zach was the friend who called me and Josh after dark to see if we wanted to sneak out and go see a midnight movie, which we only actually did once, maybe twice. Our friendship stalled when Zach transferred to a school in another district, but I still saw him every weekend at church, although at the time, he didn't want much to do with faith, and he told me so.

Josh and I embarked on our road trip in late July. We packed up my mom's red Ford Expedition with junk food and burned CDs and took off for Southern California. We followed a route that let us stay with friends of friends when we could, and we stayed in cheap motels when we couldn't. When we stopped in Fort Worth, Texas, we stayed with my friend Lindsay and her family. She and I went on our first official date at the end of freshman year and batted around the idea of dating. But it didn't pan out, mostly because I was hesitant to be tied down for the summer—a trait she didn't find endearing. Josh and I punctuated the drive with familiar faces so that even the farthest places felt close to home.

We spent some time in San Diego while I completed my short

internship, and then Josh and I drove to Chicago, where he caught a flight back to Atlanta, and I got ready for the summit. I met up with my dad, Zach, and Jim—Zach's dad—at Willow Creek Church on the morning of the first day of the conference.

Zach seemed surprisingly happy to see me. I'm not sure what happened during his freshman year at Kennesaw State, but he had experienced quite the life transformation. He was now walking the straight and narrow, and the summit was my first time seeing him since his radical conversion.

The moment I saw him, he enveloped me in a hug and said, "It's good to see you, brother." Even his language was different; any other time, he would have called me bro. He asked about the road trip, said he was bummed he didn't get to see Josh before he flew out, and told me he prayed for our safety the whole time we'd been on the road.

"Who are you, and what have you done with Zach?" I asked him, but he just laughed.

We were two of about 8,000 people at the summit, but everyone fit comfortably in the main sanctuary. The main focus was on inspiring and encouraging people to lead with diligence in their own spheres of influence. That year's lineup had eight speakers over two days, including Andy Stanley, Peg Neuhauser, Patrick Lencioni, and Bono of U2 fame. At the time, I certainly would have recognized a U2 song, but I didn't consider myself a raving fan, so I wasn't disappointed to learn that Bono wasn't actually going to be there in person. Unlike the other speakers, he had recorded a taped interview to be aired on the second day of the conference.

When it came time, the lights dimmed, and Bono's Irish accent boomed through the auditorium as he appeared on the screen: "AIDS is the single largest humanitarian crisis of our generation."

I wasn't sure whether it was the sound of his voice or the volume of the speakers, but as soon as he spoke, it felt like the air went out of the room. It seemed like everyone sat up a little straighter. Or maybe it was just me.

To say I didn't know much about AIDS would have been an understatement. My knowledge of the disease was virtually nonexistent. I'd seen the acronym in news headlines a time or two, but I didn't know anything about it beyond the fact that it was deadly. I'd never been involved in a conversation about it. In fact, I'd never even overheard a conversation about it. I was surprised to hear Bono bring it up. How did this relate to leadership?

In an interview with a pastor, Bono stated that only six percent of evangelicals felt it was incumbent on them to respond to the AIDS emergency and that he was deeply offended by that reality. He went on to say that 40 million people were living with HIV/AIDS, and 25 million of them lived in sub-Saharan Africa. He spoke of the misconceptions that branded people who'd contracted it. He said it was the leprosy of this age and quoted Scriptures describing how Christ spent his time with lepers.

"'Love thy neighbor' is not advice," he said. "It's a command."

He stated that the church, like those who came along the road before the Good Samaritan, walked across the road and looked the other way, both literally and figuratively. He asked whether that didn't contradict the very central tenets of the Scriptures we believed were true. He spoke about the extreme poverty in Africa and how that contributed to the lack of treatment and prevention. He said people were dying at an alarming rate—6,500 Africans each day.

Bono ended his interview with a challenge: The church must lead this response. Governments and NGOs couldn't address the deeper spiritual need. He said we couldn't let the church walk away from this emergency just because it was difficult, expensive, or a moral hazard. He reminded us that we were being called to care for the marginalized, isolated, and stigmatized, that everyone in the world was trying to work together to see progress in the area, and that the church not being a part of it was unacceptable. It wouldn't be acceptable in history, and it wouldn't be acceptable to God.

The screen faded to black, the lights slowly rose, and it felt as though it took a full minute for the air to come back in the room. I sat there surprised by how much I enjoyed the segment; it had been much more moving than I anticipated, and it stuck with me.

The summit was over before we knew it, and it was time for us to head back to Atlanta. We packed up early the next morning and went our separate ways—my dad and Jim to fly home and Zach and me to drive. The start of the road trip looked much like it had with Josh: The red Ford Expedition, junk food, and burned CDs were all the same, although this time, the conversations were very different.

I hadn't even pulled the car out of the hotel parking lot yet when Zach said, "We've got to go."

"Go where?" I asked. Was he hungry already?

"To Africa," he said, like it should have been obvious.

I looked over at him, and I could tell he was serious. His mouth didn't hold even a hint of a smirk.

"That's a bold declaration, even for you," I told him.

"I can't believe I didn't know the state of emergency our world is in."

"You know they usually choose an issue to highlight at the summit. Remember last year when they focused on special needs ministry and they had like a hundred kids with special needs come out and do that song?"

"I wasn't there last year."

"Well, they did—and it was incredible, by the way—but my dad told me that the year before that, they did a session about a different justice issue."

"So?" Zach asked.

"So what if that's all this was? Just a push for us to rally around a cause?"

"Then it worked," Zach said.

I pulled onto the highway and let a few exits pass by.

"What would we even do about it?" I asked. "We'd go to Africa and do what?"

"I don't know," Zach said thoughtfully. "But something more than we're doing about it right now."

"There wasn't even a clear call to action. I was moved by Bono's talk too, but it was so vague. He just said the church needs to lead the response. What does that even mean?"

I didn't mean to sound pessimistic. I was only trying to sound reasonable. But why? I'd felt something, hadn't I? I'd connected with what Bono said, even if it wasn't a conscious connection. That video was a seed, and Zach's enthusiasm was water. But the assignment felt too unclear and the issue too . . . big. Didn't Zach know that the whole notion of being able to do anything remotely helpful for the situation was unlikely?

"Maybe that's the beauty in Bono's ambiguity. Maybe there are so many things we could do that he didn't want to limit us to one idea or one approach."

"When did you get so philosophical?" I asked.

"On the road to Damascus."

I don't know what caught me off guard more—Zach's new-found life outlook or his reference to the Bible.

"We have to go to Africa as soon as we can," Zach said before I could compliment him on his Scriptural proficiency.

I wanted to write it off as impulsive, but a part of me was intrigued, like he might be on to something. That part didn't feel like me. I was the logical and levelheaded one—the one who unequivocally knew that hopping on a plane to Africa was not a responsible idea. Maybe it was Zach's zeal, which I was impressed with, if not even a little jealous of. He was so sure of and enthusiastic about his faith that he believed anything was possible. What would happen if everyone lived their lives like that?

"Zach, we're broke," I said finally. "And we don't know anything about anything. We can't just hop on a plane and try to help solve the AIDS crisis."

Or could we? There was a voice inside my head that told me not to squash the idea completely. It was only a whisper, but it was undeniable.

"How hard could it be?" Zach asked. "We'll get a video camera and go capture what's going on over there. We can make a documentary and show it to churches. At least that's a start."

Suddenly, it didn't sound so crazy. Documentaries were a great way to share information while still creating an emotional connection for people. My wheels started to turn. We'd need to hire someone to help, because we weren't experienced enough to know what to film. Would Kenyans even let us interview them? Where would we stay in Kenya? The need for a plan was apparent.

"You're overthinking things," Zach said to me. "I see it in your face."

"Someone has to," I said with a shrug.

We talked a lot more about it as we made our way home, and before long, the role of the church—or, more specifically, the lack thereof—began to dominate the conversation. We were both saddened by the state of the church as it related to the AIDS crisis. Bono had raised an interesting question: Why wasn't the church helping? If the Bible called for us to serve one another humbly in love, if we were actually commanded to love our neighbors as ourselves, why was the church turning away? Was it intentional or just a lack of awareness?

Zach and I talked about our own church. We loved our home church in Peachtree City, but like so many others, they weren't talking about the AIDS crisis, much less doing anything about it. We hadn't heard so much as a muttering about AIDS, locally or globally. Surely, there were people in our congregation who were affected by the disease, directly or indirectly. We decided it would have to start with us; we had to get our church involved somehow, even if we could just encourage them to acknowledge the fact that the disease was an issue.

When we finally arrived back in Atlanta, we felt equal parts exhausted and renewed. We'd covered so much ground and discussed many unknowns, and we both wanted to sleep for a good twelve hours before we resumed our quest for answers. As we parted ways, we confirmed that one main question had risen to the top: What would it look like for our home church, and the American church as a whole, to respond to the AIDS crisis? It was both a question and a guiding light. One that begged another important question: Where do we begin?

Those were the questions that plagued us until Thanksgiving break. Since we both went back to school in the fall—actually, I went back to school, and Zach left Kennesaw to join Impact 360, a gap year program that taught biblical education and community-based discipleship—we didn't meet up again until we were both back home in November. In the months since the summit, the conclusion we had come to was that we wanted to focus specifically on Kenya. Zach was the one to bring that idea to the table, and he was adamant about it. It was a highly affected country in a safe part of the continent, and he felt God was leading us there.

I ensured we did our due diligence by researching different organizations that worked in a similar space, whether AIDS relief, African development, or social justice. We looked into what World Vision International, Invisible Children, Aid for Africa, and International Justice Mission were doing and what results they were getting. In doing so, we noticed a common starting point: awareness. Those organizations were multifaceted, and they had countless resources, donors, grants, employees, and influence, but before any donation was given or service provided, people had to know and care about a cause. These organizations provided awareness to the masses about an issue—or, in some cases, multiple issues. This all affirmed Zach's idea of starting with a documentary.

Prior to the summit, Zach and I had been blissfully unaware of the growing epidemic in Africa, so we assumed many others were also in the dark on the subject. We could be the ones to tell them. We could spread the word to people and churches about what was going on.

By the end of our Thanksgiving break, we had made up our minds: We were going to film a documentary in Kenya about the AIDS crisis. We didn't know much beyond that, but we had until summer break to figure it out. In the next six months, we had to raise money to pay for the cost of our trip, hire a videographer who would work for dirt cheap and agree to fly across the world with college students, make arrangements for whatever accommodations were available in Kenya, and convince Josh to go with us.

After we announced our plan to family and friends, my mom and dad sat me down.

"Son," my dad said, "we'd feel a lot better about your trip if you could get somebody on the ground to help you. Someone who knows their way around Kenya. Someone who could be your guide. We both know the value of having somebody in front of you who's walked there before."

My mom seconded this suggestion: "We don't want you to do any of this alone. You might have one good brain between you."

My dad mentioned that Jim knew a man whose daughter did ministry work in Kenya, and he offered to connect us. Her name was Kim Pace, and Zach and I went to meet her when we were back in town over Christmas break. She was older than us, though not by much, and she turned out to be a rich source of knowledge, our real saving grace.

We gave her some background on what drove us to want to go to Kenya to make a documentary about AIDS and shared the specifics of our plans related to visiting different villages and interviewing people who were living with the disease. We told her we'd also love to speak with some pastors to get a sense of what Kenyan churches were doing to respond to the crisis.

"I run a ministry out of Brackenhurst, in Limuru, right outside of Nairobi," Kim said. "I know two guys who graduated from the seminary there, and they are both passionate about AIDS; I think they'd be the perfect guys to help you. They can be your translators, which you'll definitely need, and they can help you deal with Kenyan transportation so you end up getting where you want to go. They work for me when they're not in the field doing ministry, and I don't mind if you hire them for the time you're there. All I'd ask is that you supplement their income and pay them for their help."

Once we agreed on a price, she said she'd make the arrangements. We thanked her profusely and left the meeting feeling such gratitude. It felt as though things were starting to fall into place. Now we needed to concentrate on raising money. Josh said he'd help us design a letter that laid out the vision God had given us so we could send it to people and ask for their support. As the three of us worked on it together, Josh fully caught our vision and became our trip photographer and the third member of our travel team.

From then until summer, we sent out our letters to family, friends, and friends of friends. We met with potential donors and shared, to the best of our understanding, what God was leading us to do. It was through one of those secondary connections that we were introduced to a videographer named Jon. He was a young guy looking for experience and adventure, and after a handful of conversations with him, he became our official fourth. Miraculously, we reached our monetary goal. We would be able to purchase four plane tickets and a backup video camera and still have money for transportation, lodging, food, and our guides.

God opened every door that led to Kenya. It wasn't something we took lightly; we knew full well the blessing we'd been given and knew that we needed to be responsible with what we did with it. As the four of us boarded our flight to Nairobi in late May, we waved goodbye to our parents, our American conveniences, our preconceived notions, and our old lives. Even though we didn't know what the outcome of the trip would be, we knew it would change us. We knew we'd leave the US as one person and come back another. And we were right.

# CHAPTER SIX

# CORNEL

Kim Pace was the one who introduced us to the four Americans. We met Kim several years before, when she started a ministry at Brackenhurst for the children of missionaries. She hosted activities for them like ropes courses and summer camps for them to attend when their parents were away doing ministry work. When Duncan and I graduated from seminary, Kim asked if we wanted to work for her as facilitators. It looked like her work was fun. I had seen many people in trees over the months and thought they looked too human to be monkeys. I was grateful for the opportunity. Even though my heart wanted to carry out the vision Duncan and I had to work with those who suffered from AIDS, I needed to make money to send home to Kisumu. My heart would have to wait.

At first, Duncan and I lived in staff housing at Brackenhurst, in a shared room with other facilitators. But we desired more space so we moved to Ruaka, about thirty kilometers east. Neither of us had a lot of money to spare, especially me because I was saving for my wedding. We went as far as Ruaka because it was more affordable. We had lived within the seminary compound for many years, so it was a nice change to be in the open world. It was also nice for Duncan's son, George. There were other children near our small one-room home. And neighbors kept an eye on him when we were at work.

Duncan and I received a message from Kim while she was in America doing a fundraising effort. She said filmmakers were coming to Kenya to get footage about AIDS. She had told them about us. They would be here for close to one month. We should host them and take them around to interview people in areas where HIV was prevalent. When we were in Nairobi, we could stay in her home as she would not be in the country at that time. We would be paid the same wages as though we were working for her.

That sounded good to me. I was pleased to combine the topic of AIDS with the familiar work of guiding and translating for Americans. For the next five months, Duncan and I worked together to plan their trip. We had gotten to know many patients, pastors, and clinics since our conversation under the tree in Tanzania. We spent much of our available time speaking to youth about True Love Waits, a movement that encourages them to abstain. We visited people who were HIV positive and prayed with them, made sure they had access to medication, offered to take them to church, and met with the families of those who allowed us. After the message from Kim, we reached out to those people on behalf of the Americans and arranged for interviews.

On the day they arrived, Duncan and I went to the airport with a sign. *Justin Miller* was all it read. That was the extent of what we knew about him and the others.

We waited outside of baggage claim and looked right past the four teenagers who came out of the double doors full of youthful energy. One had his fists in the air and shouted, "We made it!" and then high-fived the others.

*Jorochere mamor*, excited tourists, I thought. I was shocked when they walked toward us. It had never crossed my mind that we were not waiting for four adults.

"Duncan?" one of them asked me.

"Justin?" I asked in return.

"I'm Zach," he said. He was the one who had his hands in the air seconds earlier.

"I am Cornel," I told him. "That there is Duncan."

We all exchanged handshakes. Zach, Josh, Jon, and Justin. Each of them looked like the other, and I wondered if I would be able to keep them straight.

"Is there an adult with you?" Duncan asked as he looked behind them.

"What? No," Justin said. His look was of pride and surprise.

"Transportation is this way," I said and reached for one of their bags.

"No, thanks, Duncan," Zach said. "I got it."

We took a taxi from the airport to Kim's home in Westlands. It was about twenty kilometers away. But due to our roads and traffic, the trip took longer than they expected. The teenagers talked the whole time and very fast. They seemed more eager than any traveler I had met before. Duncan and I tried to keep up with their many questions.

"Hey, do you know people in government? Can we go to their offices?"

"No, we cannot speak to them just like that."

"Can we visit a hospital? Do you guys have a certain ward for people with AIDS?"

"We do not have what you call a 'ward' but we can take you to a hospital."

"Will we be able to interview a prostitute?"

That one gave us pause. "Perhaps we can try to arrange something."

It was late when we arrived at Kim's home. It was very

generous of her to allow us to stay there and a wonderful way to welcome our guests. There was room for everyone to sleep comfortably. Since it was an expatriate home, it had modern conveniences like electricity and running water. It even had a television and a Nintendo GameCube, which produced great enthusiasm from our new American friends. I wanted to warn them of the misleading standard set by Kim's home. But I knew they would soon figure it out for themselves.

We stayed in Nairobi for the first few days of their trip. We took them to see some slums, starting with one within walking distance of Brackenhurst. Jon had his video camera, Josh had his camera for photos, Zach had his hat that read, "Jesus is my homie," whatever that meant, and Justin had his notebook with all the questions they wanted to ask. We walked down the narrow dirt road in the center of the slum. They boldly walked up to people to try to begin conversations. I think they mistook curious stares for invitations. Duncan and I quickly cut in. We knew most residents would not know English. We also knew that even if they did, they would not want to discuss AIDS so openly with strangers.

In Swahili, I explained about the film and asked if anyone would be willing to speak with the filmmakers. There may have been one or two who agreed. But I cannot say that the first day was successful. Many were wary of the foreigners. Others were uncomfortable with the topic. I saw the discouragement on Justin's face.

"Tomorrow we will visit some people in a private setting," I told him. "They have already agreed to speak with you."

The next day, we took them to Huruma Baptist Church, the same church where Duncan first found his son, George. We introduced our guests to the pastor, who was very pleased to have American visitors and to exercise his English. With the camera recording, they spoke with him about the stigma placed upon those who were HIV positive and wanted to know if he welcomed those who were infected into his church. Were they allowed to worship alongside others?

"Yes, my sons. But I am afraid that their immediate needs are not spiritual."

"What are their immediate needs?" Justin asked.

"Food and medicine. And jobs."

We met with a man who served in the church and who talked about the amount of orphans in the area. He said there were too many to count, these children whose parents died of AIDS and had nowhere to go. Many of them were looked upon as carriers of the disease and were not welcomed into their neighbors' homes. Some tried to find their way to other villages so people would not pass judgment upon them so immediately.

We sat down with a member of the congregation who was a Luo and who had requested that I translate. Her eyes looked to the ground as she told me how she lost two small children to AIDS and carried much guilt over being the one who gave it to them. She cried as Zach asked if she knew how she came to be infected.

"I do not know how I got it. I have been faithful," she told me.

They asked how she was able to survive. Was she on treatment?

"I have stopped taking medicine," she said. "I wish to go be with my children."

As we left the church, there was a change in the energy of Justin and the others.

"This is heavy," Zach said.

Justin's expression echoed the sentiment.

"It's all so complicated," said Josh.

Duncan and I took them to get something to eat. We knew they were focused on the pain they had just heard. We wished to provide them with some comfort. Duncan discussed the progress in the region and how it used to be that churches automatically turned those with AIDS away. Now they were allowed to attend and were openly lifted up in prayer. He did not mention how that did not apply to every church. Or that those who welcomed them in often made them sit in a pew in the back.

I was proud of Duncan for giving the Americans hope, especially since the relationship between AIDS and the church was a sensitive topic for him. His father remained resistant to embracing the sick into his congregation. He believed that people either contracted the disease due to promiscuity or as a punishment for sin. Either way, it was a sinful disease that he did not want to spread.

Kisumu was the next location on our schedule. We boarded a large bus. Every seat was filled with at least one person. It was very warm outside and even warmer inside. The bus ride took eight hours. The excited teenagers from the airport now seemed less enthusiastic. Jon's phone was not getting service. Josh had many mosquito bites, although Nairobi mosquitos did not have the appetite of Kisumu mosquitos, which caused me to worry for him. Zach was hungry. Justin was surprised by the poor condition of the roads. *Waruaki Kenya*, welcome to Kenya.

I was seated next to Justin, but it was as if we shared a seat.

"I'm glad we got to meet that pastor yesterday," he said as he tried to encourage a bug to go out the window. "We'd definitely like to speak with more since we want this documentary to communicate to the American church that there are churches and pastors in these communities who are well positioned to help meet some of the needs, but they don't have enough resources to help with everything. At least not on their own."

"Yes, we shall meet with more. We are staying with a pastor in Eldoret, as a matter of fact."

"How do you feel the climate is right now with how members of the congregation view people with AIDS?"

"Climate?"

"The setting, the mood. Do they welcome people with AIDS into the church if the pastor does? Or are they skeptical?"

"I think they respond in the way the pastor does. If the pastor is fine with it, they are more likely to be fine with it."

"So if we want to change people's minds, it starts with the pastor." He did not say it as a question.

"What started your interest in HIV/AIDS?" I asked.

"Zach and I went to a conference with our dads last summer and heard Bono speak. Do you know him?"

"No, I have not had the pleasure. Is he from Kenya?"

"No, he's a musician. In a band called U2?"

I shook my head.

"He's passionate about the AIDS crisis over here, and he spoke at the conference about how the American church doesn't do enough to help."

"Do you agree?"

"From what I can tell, he's right. At least the churches I'm familiar with. But there is so much potential for what they could do if they all just did something—anything."

He opened his mouth to say something more but then stopped. As if he was choosing his words carefully.

"It would be easy to just blame the church," he said finally. "But I have to take responsibility for my own ignorance. I'm embarrassed to say that until last year, I didn't really know what AIDS was."

"You cannot hold yourself accountable over something you did not know."

"I'm committed now to making sure as many people know as possible. Once they do, they'll feel compelled to do something."

He was a remarkable young man and very caring. "I am blessed to know you, Justin."

When we arrived in Kisumu, it was much hotter than in Nairobi. We went to a hostel to secure our beds. The next morning, we made the long journey from Kisumu town to Seka, my home village. As we got closer and closer to my family's land, Zach began to point to the Xs that were painted above doors. We stopped so Jon could film them. Maybe they did not have those in America.

I had not been home for several months. I had written my mother a letter telling her I was coming home with guests, and I could tell it had been received. She was wearing a dress reserved for Sundays and had prepared a meal. She killed a chicken for us that morning and made *sukuma wiki kod ugali*, collard greens and cornmeal porridge. When we walked in, she blessed us with a prayer and brought around a pitcher of water so we could clean our hands before eating.

My father came in then. I was surprised to see how very thin he had become. I greeted him and saw up close that he looked much older than he had months before. He was not overly friendly to the guests, although I did not expect he would be. He took his food outside while we finished our meal and spoke with my mother.

We got back to the hostel and slept two to a bed in beds that were meant for one. It was very warm inside the room. Josh taught me the new word stuffy. The boys said much to Duncan and me about how the mosquito nets made it hard for them to breathe. But we did not think they would like the alternative.

Over the next few days, we were at last able to speak with people who were HIV positive. We took bicycle taxis to travel from meeting to meeting. The Americans appreciated the wind from the open bicycles. Duncan and I switched back and forth as translators, although there were some times when English could be used. Justin and Zach were the ones to ask the questions while Jon filmed and Josh took photographs. Sometimes Josh also asked questions. Many subjects asked that we meet in the privacy of their homes as to not draw unwanted attention. It had been a long time since they had visitors. I sensed they were both anxious and grateful.

We met with a married couple who both had AIDS. They were the only two I knew who stood united in their status. Their children played on the floor during the interview because they were too weak to lift them. The husband and wife said that they lived in total darkness, surrounded by the cloud of death. When Justin asked what that meant for their family, they said all of their worry lived around who will care for their children.

We spoke to a young mother who had been kicked out of her home by her husband after testing positive. She and her child now lived with her widowed father. But he drew a line down the center of the room they shared that she was not permitted to cross. Zach asked if she knew how she got HIV. She said she believed it was a punishment from the Lord for not properly honoring her parents as a young girl.

We interviewed a woman who was covered in scabs and who seemed very close to death. She lived far away from others in a home that was made of *mabati*, iron sheet. It was on the edge of a swamp. She said her father built it for her after her husband kicked her out for being too sickly. He did not care that she was pregnant with his child. Once she had been officially diagnosed, she was fired from her job. She delivered the baby a couple of months later. But he died at one year because of his HIV status.

We sat at the bedside of a young man who said a pastor had promised him healing. He sold his belongings for 3,000 shillings, about US$30, in order to pay the pastor to pray over him. Afterward, the pastor brought somebody out from the back who tested the young man and told him he was now HIV negative. He stopped taking his medication and was now too close to death for doctors to help.

There were many interviews in Kisumu, too many to save to memory. It was just over a week into their trip. Justin, Zach,

Josh, and Jon already seemed very tired. It was not the need for sleep but more the need for quiet. Duncan and I thought they would like familiar American food before we went back to the hostel to rest. We took them to eat sandwiches with beef that are called burgers. They seemed uncertain when they saw the establishment. But we assured them they would be fine.

We were headed back to our hostel after our meal when we walked past some prostitutes. I recalled that the Americans had asked to talk to one at the same time Justin whispered to me, "We would love the opportunity to interview a prostitute." When I saw Zach whisper to Duncan, I assumed it was the same request. I knew we were not going back to the hostel just yet.

I understood why they wanted to speak with someone in that industry. HIV affected the lives of those women whether they had the disease or not. The risk was always there. I did not know what kind of reaction we would get from asking them about it. We took the four boys aside and Duncan told them, "If you tell them you are there to do an interview, they will never talk to you. You have to tell them that you want their services and then negotiate a price."

Their eyes all got very wide.

"We will choose one for you who knows English and is used to working with Americans," I said.

Duncan continued, "Then ask her if you can pay her that price but instead of her typical services, ask if you could just talk to her and hear her story."

Justin was chosen by his friends as the one to approach her, and I told him I would be one pace behind him. His nervousness made him seem even younger than he was. He walked slowly up to the woman whom Duncan and I had pointed out.

"I'm visiting Kisumu on a trip, and I'm looking to have a good time," Justin said. He told me later that was the only thing he could think of to say.

"Well, I could show you a good time," she said.

He was hesitant when he said, "Okay, great. Sounds fun. How much?"

"For an hour, six US dollars."

"Okay, I'd like to pay you that, but instead of whatever it is we were going to do, I want to buy you a soda or dinner."

She looked very confused.

He looked behind him to where I was standing, then looked back to her and kept talking. "If you'd let us, we'd like to interview you for a documentary we're making about HIV. We would love to hear about how it affects your life." He pointed to where Duncan stood with Jon, Josh, Zach, and the video camera. She looked at them, at me, and then back to Justin before she agreed.

"Soliciting a prostitute. That's a first for me," Justin quietly told me as we walked her to a bar. "And a last."

Her name was Ann. She spoke openly to Justin about her life and what had led her to where she was. She said that HIV had only become a concern to her five years ago, when some of her friends began to die. She often asked her clients beforehand if they had it. But no one had ever said yes. And no matter, she said. Even if a client was infected, she had little choice about protection. This job was not a job of choice but a job made from the lack of choices. It was the only option to feed her children, so what she thought about HIV made no difference.

Justin was quiet for a moment after she said these things, so she stared at him. She then asked him about a colored bracelet he wore around his wrist. He told her it was a gospel bracelet. He went one by one through each color and shared with her what it meant.

After the interview, Zach introduced me to Red Bull. I had three of them before we left the bar. We rode tuk-tuks, auto rickshaws, back to the hostel, where we could finally rest. When we got there, Zach noticed he no longer had his notebook. It was the one that kept track of everything they filmed and had what they called annotated minutes. Based on their reaction, out of all the notebooks to lose, that one was not the best choice.

"I swear I had it," Zach said. "I got on the tuk-tuk with it."

"We captured the timestamps of every single interview in there. How do you just lose a three-ring binder?" Justin asked.

"It must have fallen out while we were driving," Zach said.

"Let us go and look for it," I said. "Duncan and Josh, perhaps you go look for the tuk-tuk driver to see if it was left with him. I will go with the others to walk the path from where we came."

We walked back and forth along the dirt road. It was dark and very hard to see without lights. Then it began to rain.

"If it is out here, it's now in a puddle," Justin said. Just then, a car drove in our direction. Its headlights showed both sides of the road in full view. Off to the right, not far from where we got on the tuk-tuks, was the notebook. Zach ran over and picked it up.

"It's all here, everything's here! It's just a little wet."

"Crisis averted," Jon said when the three of us gathered around Zach.

We got back to the hostel for the second time that night and intended to go straight to sleep. Unfortunately, my reaction to the Red Bull was very poor. It caused me to feel very awake and *mirimiri*, shaky. It also caused a pain in my stomach. As the others got into bed with their mosquito nets, I went to the common area, where they had a television set. There was a football match on. The Red Bull caused me to be very *mbachni*, mesmerized.

I do not know how long I was watching when Justin ran into the common area and said he was concerned about Zach. I followed him into the room we all shared and saw Zach as a small round ball in the corner. As I got closer, I saw he was sweating. His whole body looked wet. It was not just because it was stuffy.

"I feel like my stomach is going to explode," Zach said without opening his eyes. He said it a few more times and got louder each time. I thought it was maybe because of the Red Bull, as that was similar to how my stomach felt. But when I looked around to the others, I saw they too did not look well. Josh and Jon were sweating and looked to be even whiter than normal. Duncan had his hand over his stomach. Justin looked fine, just scared.

It was believed that everyone besides Justin had food poisoning. I was surprised that I too had a reaction to the burgers. My stomach was used to eating anything I could find. Some things I ate growing up were not even meant to be eaten. Zach was in the worst condition, so we took him to the hospital. They gave him some fluids and a shot in his behind, with a very large needle. We went back to the hostel for the third time that night and slept for only one or two hours before we had to go to the bus station.

We all climbed onto one tuk-tuk and stacked our bags in the back. When we arrived at the station and unloaded our things, Justin's large hiking backpack was no longer on top of the pile. Not only were his clothes, personal supplies, and a camera in there, but it also held the rest of their money. Over US$1,000.

"Guys, we have to go find it," he said. He was very panicked.

The tuk-tuk driver agreed to take them back toward the hostel while Duncan and I went to the village we had just passed to see if anyone found it. While on the tuk-tuk, Justin saw someone on a bicycle wearing the backpack. They pulled to the side of the road and told the rider how that was their backpack and thanked him for finding it. He began to take it off as a small crowd formed. Most Kenyans are curious when they see white people.

"He is the one who found it," a woman in the crowd said. "He deserves to be paid."

"Actually I am the one who found it first," a man said. "I deserve to be paid too."

Others in the crowd began yelling. Duncan and I heard it and spotted our four friends in the middle. We ran as fast as we could and tried to calm people down. The boys were very unsure of what to do. I looked at Justin and hoped he understood my eyes that told him not to open the backpack or let them see his money. I took some cash out of my pocket and gave it to the man on the bicycle. Duncan took the backpack and encouraged the crowd to go away. We slowly made our way out of the center of the circle and walked back to the bus station.

Justin looked at Duncan and me and said, "The last twelve hours have been rough. It feels like the wheels are falling off."

I did not know what that meant. But I could see from his face that his heart was heavy. "It will be okay, my friend," I told him.

"We still have half your trip to go. We will have a lot of fun," Duncan said.

I knew if the Americans ever came back, I would have to give them a better experience in my home city of Kisumu than that one. We got to the bus station for the second time that day and boarded a bus to Eldoret. Everyone slept on the four-hour ride. We were to stay with a local pastor, so we walked to his home after our bus arrived.

The pastor lived among many other homes. The neighbors greeted us warmly when we got there. We saw the pastor as he stood in his doorway, wearing a hat that read, "Absolutely, positively, definitely stoned." We do not believe he knew what that meant.

He introduced us to his family. We spent the next few days enjoying the community in which he lived. We played many games of football with the children who lived in the surrounding neighborhoods. We watched the news from a small television set that was plugged into a car battery. The pastor's home was made of cinder blocks and had cement floors, so it stayed very cool, which pleased the Americans. They were also grateful for the small indoor room dedicated to showers. We poured buckets of water over ourselves. It was the cleanest our group had been in a week.

The pastor lived near other church officials as well. We shared several meals together and spoke with them about how fast AIDS had spread through western Kenya. They told us of the divide between churches in the area. They estimated that half allowed the sick to attend services while the other half did not.

"What's their rationale for not allowing the sick?" Zach asked.

"There are some who believe it is spread through air or touch," one official said.

"Even those who know better still fear it," said the pastor.

"Fear the disease or fear the association?" Justin asked.

"Both," the pastor replied.

"Does your church help those who are HIV positive?"

"Help in what way?"

"Food or employment or transportation to get to the doctor?"

"No, unfortunately we do not have those things to give."

We stayed in a small town outside Eldoret called Bungoma before returning to Nairobi for the rest of their trip. We had a very busy last week. We took the Americans to meet with and interview staff members of agencies who worked in the area of AIDS. We snuck into a hospital and spoke to a nurse who told us that many who were HIV positive go untreated because after they find out their status, they are too ashamed to go back and see the doctor. We interviewed another prostitute who said she felt trapped by her work but had no other way to provide for her family. When Zach asked her about AIDS, she said she knew it was a risk of the job. She tried to get her clients to wear condoms. But many refused. She had never been tested. We visited an orphanage where the headmaster said that hundreds of children lost their parents to AIDS every month. She turned them away daily since the shelter was already over capacity.

After these interviews, a Bungoma pastor decided he needed the Americans to preach at his congregation. He would not take no for an answer. Our guests learned many things that week in

Bungoma, even that the color of their skin came with the expectation of either money or ministry, neither of which they felt prepared or adequate to give.

The emotions of our four guests went up and down. We saw in them sadness and hope. Worry and courage. Doubt and passion. Duncan and I understood how they felt because we had often experienced those emotions ourselves. It was helpful to stay at Kim's home because it provided *kar yueyo*, solace. For the last day of their trip, it was decided that we would relax around her home in preparation for their flight back to America that evening.

Justin was the first American to rise in the morning. He joined me and Duncan at the table for coffee. We asked his thoughts about the trip as a whole and of his intentions once he arrived back in the US.

"We'll definitely make the documentary, but last night we were talking about how maybe this is more than just a documentary. Change requires more than a film."

"You said before that you wanted to educate people. That is what your film can do," I told Justin.

"Yes, it will be more than what a lot of other people are doing," Duncan said.

"Now I think maybe a documentary is not enough. You guys know this crisis; you have been doing this work already. What would you do if you were in our shoes? How can the church around the world help end the AIDS crisis?"

We were not in the shoes of Justin, or Zach or Jon or Josh. But we did know what we wanted to do.

"It is a long answer, Justin. But we have written everything down," I told him.

"Maybe if you want, we can show you our proposal," Duncan said. "We would like to start a ministry called Oasis of Endless Hope. We intend to present the plan to churches so they can see their role in how to support those with HIV. You can read through it so that you might understand."

"Okay, where's the proposal?"

"It is at our home."

"Can we go get it?"

Duncan and I looked at each other. "You can take him," I said. "I will stay here with the others."

They took a matatu to our neighborhood, which was thirty minutes away. Duncan said that Justin was very surprised when he saw where we lived. It was a single room that did not even have an indoor bathroom. Justin had thought we had a place like Kim's. Duncan showed him our eight pages of proposal. Justin asked to keep it. Since it was our only copy, they stopped at a shopping center to make photocopies on their way back to Limuru. They also drove by the home where Duncan and I wished to open our ministry offices and run our operations.

"With a home like we have right now in Ruaka," Duncan told him, "no one will ever meet with us or trust us. But in a centralized place, pastors and people would come, and they would listen, and we would share with them."

"What will it take to make it happen?" Justin asked.

"Prayer."

Justin laughed. "No, I mean financially."

"You know, this is a very expensive program model. What we would need to run the ministry, including the renting of the home, would be $200 a month."

"I see," said Justin.

They joined us back at Kim's home. We all ate lunch together while we discussed the events of the past few weeks. It had been a very full trip, with many people and places. They told us their eyes had been opened to the destruction of HIV. They were happy to be going home but felt that their work in Kenya was unfinished.

"That makes sense," Duncan said. "You have not even begun to make your documentary yet."

"It's more than that," Justin said. The others nodded as if they knew what he was going to say. "We don't know what to do with all we've seen."

I did not know what to say. And whenever I did not have the words, I relied on the Holy Word. "I tell you the truth. Anything you did for even the least of my people here, you also did for me."

When we dropped them off at the airport, we hugged one another and said goodbye. On the bus ride back to our home, both Duncan and I were very grateful to have made four new friends. But in all of our honesty, we never thought we would see or hear from them again.

# CHAPTER SEVEN

# JUSTIN

I put their proposal in my carry-on so I could read it again during the flight home. I ended up reading it five more times, once every few hours. I was impressed by the thought and care they'd so obviously poured into it; it was multifaceted, tactical, and all around smart. I thought the name Oasis of Endless Hope needed some work—although it was better than the original name that was crossed out at the top of the proposal, METLWA: Ministry and Evangelism through True Love Waits AIDS ministry—but they weren't far off with the rest. They were both invested in doing something to make a difference.

Based on all the arrangements they'd made for us on our trip, I knew they were well informed about the AIDS crisis. They had spouted off stats and spoken of the history of the disease, they provided insights and thoughts about perceptions and hurdles, and they were certainly connected to a huge network of people who were either infected or affected by the disease. Their network of pastors alone seemed endless.

Their proposal even included providing education to the church and the patients themselves. They wanted to educate pastors, who could in turn educate their congregations about AIDS. By doing so, those who were HIV positive would be accepted into the church and its community, which was important not only for spiritual growth but also for fellowship; they did not want people who were fighting for their lives to feel more isolated than they already did.

The biggest component of their strategy, though, involved counseling HIV patients. They reasoned that many people who were HIV positive did not take medication, or if they did, they didn't take it correctly. Cornel and Duncan wanted an organization to advise patients on treatment plans, teach them about nutrition, and show them how to strengthen their immune systems. They wanted patients to feel informed, but more than that, they wanted patients to feel supported.

I didn't show the plan to Zach, Josh, or Jon right away. I would, eventually, but on that flight home, we all had too much on our minds already. My mind wouldn't rest, even without the proposal swirling around in it. It was going to take time to properly reflect on everything I'd experienced and figure out how I felt about it. I kept playing scenes of the trip over and over again in my head: the deserted homes with Xs above the doors, the frail twenty-something crying in his hospital bed, the gratitude from Ann when I simply bought her dinner, the pastor who stood at the church door on Sunday morning and welcomed every single person by name, the mounds of dirt signaling freshly dug graves, the white house with the caged windows that Duncan and Cornel wanted for their ministry offices, Pamela dying of loneliness and cast to the edge of her community. They were all things I would never unsee.

When we finally landed in Atlanta, it felt so good to be home. I spent the first few days sleeping off the jet lag and spending time with my parents and David. I looked around at my family and felt very grateful. Even though I was always grateful for them, I felt especially content after that trip. I always knew that we had each other's backs, come what may, but now I knew without question that millions of people around the world couldn't say the same.

I was also thrilled to get to talk to Lindsay on the phone again, and we spoke for hours on end. After that ill-fated date our freshman year, we settled into a close friendship. That friendship turned into more during our sophomore year, when she became my girlfriend.

Once our waking hours started to return to normal, we jumped into sorting through the footage from our trip. It took countless hours to review it all, particularly because it was shot on cassette tapes instead of digital files. Zach and Josh were at my house around the clock as we threw ourselves into learning Final Cut Pro. We were way out of our league.

We worked on piecing it together for two months straight. Being so engrossed in the content naturally prompted a lot of reflection and discussion between us about the trip. I finally shared Cornel and Duncan's proposal with the others, and we read it back and forth to each other, trying to find holes, as if looking for a concrete reason—any reason—to not be a part of it. The thing was, Cornel and Duncan hadn't given it to me so I could be a part of it. They hadn't asked for my help or even my opinion. They gave it to me because I asked to see it. The fact that I couldn't get it out of my head was on me, not them.

At the beginning of August, we completed our project. Our dreams of producing a documentary feature film that showed the reality of the AIDS epidemic, explained the immediacy of the situation, pierced the hearts of evangelicals, and made Americans want to respond to the humanitarian crisis turned out to be an eight-minute trailer. It wasn't what we set out to make, but we told ourselves that a full-length version could be just down the road. All things considered, we were proud of the end result. We were especially proud that we finished it by the time we headed back to school—at least we'd stuck to our timeline. The planner in me was grateful for the win.

We showed it to several pastors in the area and asked if they would be willing to partner with a Kenyan church that couldn't afford to properly support their HIV-positive congregants and community members. Most were polite but few took us seriously. They told us they weren't taking new partners or that AIDS wasn't their area of focus, and while that may have been true, I couldn't help but feel their responses had more to do with our inadequacies. We didn't have names of Kenyan churches that needed assistance. We didn't have an itemized budget of where the money would go. We didn't have materials to leave with them so they could share the information with their church leaders. All we had was an eight-minute video that featured interview clips and footage of suffering Kenyan communities, all set to powerful music. In our desperation to get the American church involved as quickly as possible, we hadn't taken the time to work out a strategy for what came next.

That fall, I joined Vanderbilt's study-abroad program in Dublin. Three other friends who were all studying abroad in different countries flew with me to Europe two weeks before the semester began to travel around together. We were staying in a small apartment in Cinque Terre, Italy, when the residual exhaustion from the trip to Kenya finally subsided. As I sat on a balcony looking out at the Ligurian Sea, what can only be described as peace rushed over me, and I felt assurance placed on my heart. I felt it so deeply and so clearly that it was almost audible:

*This is something I put in front of you, and I'm asking you to be obedient. I want you to take the next step and say yes to what Cornel and Duncan need.*

That kind of experience wasn't something that happened to me often, if ever. I'd never felt guided in such a deliberate way, and I didn't dare question it. I sat in that assurance for a minute, and then I took out my phone and dialed Duncan's number.

"Hello, my American friend," his voice boomed. "This is the first time I am receiving a telephone call from an international number!"

"Duncan, it's so good to hear you! I haven't been at peace since I left Kenya." I took a deep breath. "Until now," I added. "I want to help you and Cornel with Oasis of Endless Hope."

I winced a little when I said the name. It still didn't sit right with me, but I took the silence on the other end of the line as a sign to keep talking.

"Your plan is great; the only thing missing is the money. If all you need is $200 a month to be able to start, I can help with that. I can make sure you have $200 a month. You should sign the papers for the lease on the house."

Still there was silence.

"Duncan?" I asked.

"It is a miracle, Justin," he exclaimed. "This is very exciting!"

I wasn't exactly sure how I was going to get them $200 a month, but I'd figure something out, even if it meant taking it from my own personal savings, not going out to eat for the rest of my college career, or fundraising on their behalf.

"I will go share the news with Cornel. I cannot believe it," Duncan said.

He thanked me a half dozen times and said he'd call after they secured the house. We hung up, and I sat there, stunned. I couldn't believe what I'd just done, mostly because I did it without a plan for how I would deliver on my promise. I didn't know if that meant I was exhibiting faithfulness or recklessness.

My next two phone calls were to my parents and Kim Pace. My dad said he was proud of my initiative, and my mom said she was sending me a hug through the phone. When I called Kim, she was elated. She knew even more than I did how much this meant to Duncan and Cornel, and she became our go-between. Since they didn't have bank accounts yet, Kim received and passed along the initial monthly payment. She helped them review the leasing agreement for the house, and she made sure they wrote up an itemized budget and kept receipts. Kim was a godsend for all of us.

The next few months were a blur. In addition to finding money to send to Kenya and keeping up with my classwork, there was someone either passing through or coming into Dublin for a visit almost every weekend. Still, I made sure to connect with Cornel and Duncan a few times a month. At that point, they were setting up their offices and establishing the infrastructure of the program. They still worked as facilitators for Kim, all the while hoping that, one day, there would be enough growth for them to take a salary and dedicate themselves full time to their new ministry—which now had a much better name: CARE for AIDS. The four of us—Cornel, Duncan, Zach, and me—all agreed on the new name and moved to register as an official organization. In order to file the incorporation documents with the state, we needed to build a board of directors, so Zach and I reached out to our various connections—or, more accurately, our dads' various connections—and put together a group that included a pastor, a marketing expert, and a finance guy.

Duncan and Cornel ran the day-to-day operations in Kenya from the CARE for AIDS house—which we referred to as the White House (for its color as much as its power). They started inviting people who were HIV positive to meet with them two times each week. Before long, they had forty-five women who came to each meeting, and it became like a group therapy session. The women were able to share their experiences with one another while Duncan and Cornel served tea and presided over the topics of conversation. Over the course of a few months, they also began inviting select pastors to attend.

At first, the pastors came to the meetings as keynote speakers, and some of the women were suspicious; they had been rejected by churches in their community because of their HIV status, something they assumed was a direct consequence of the pastors' judgment. Cornel and Duncan reassured the women that the pastors were there to encourage them and pray for them, not to pass judgment on them. As the weeks went on, the presence and kindness of the pastors softened the suspicions of the women. Some who had never gone to church in the first place found faith for the first time at those meetings.

As for the pastors, they were always shocked by the turnout. Cornel and Duncan soon asked forward-thinking pastors to host similar types of meetings at their own churches. The pastors wouldn't have to run the meetings, just allow them to take place in their church compounds. Imagine all the people CARE for AIDS could reach if they weren't limited to just one meeting place. Despite how supportive they seemed of what Duncan and Cornel were doing, most pastors remained hesitant, and of the dozen pastors who attended White House meetings, only one showed willingness to host at his own church.

That church was Imani Baptist, and the first pilot program of CARE for AIDS officially launched there in January 2008. It had the same agenda as the White House meeting—sharing, camaraderie, and tea—just at a new location. Cornel and Duncan oversaw a small and incredibly talented staff of three, Rosemary, Humphrey, and Kevin, who helped counsel clients in spiritual matters, as well as matters pertaining to health and medication. The most profound difference was the number of people—more than a hundred HIV-positive men and women showed up at the first meeting at Imani. That was when Duncan and Cornel knew for certain that CARE for AIDS was on to something. There was nothing else like it; there was no other place where people could go to feel welcomed, enlightened, and heard. But then, unfortunately, it all came to a pause.

I was back stateside, starting the second semester of my junior year with a full agenda: I was still in the fraternity, I was practicing and traveling with the Ultimate team, and I was taking my maximum class load to earn a double major. Meanwhile, I was also fundraising to sustain CARE for AIDS, overseeing the board of directors, and getting more serious in my relationship with Lindsay. It was an extremely busy time for me, but it was nothing compared to what Cornel and Duncan were working through.

Their tribes, Kikuyu and Luo, had a long history of discord, particularly pertaining to politics. In 1964, shortly after Kenya gained independence from Britain, a Kikuyu man was elected as Kenya's first president. Since that time, there had been only two other sitting presidents, one of whom was also Kikuyu. The Kikuyu tribe, to which Duncan belonged, was the largest tribe in Kenya, so their dominance over civilian votes made sense. It also meant politicians from the Luo tribe, Cornel's tribe, always represented the opposition. Although the Luos were passionate, persuasive, and willing to put up a good fight, they always lost in a vote.

In 2007, as Kikuyu president Mwai Kibaki's first term was coming to an end, a Luo man by the name of Raila Odinga made his second bid for president. Early opinion polls indicated that Odinga was going to pull off a win, empowering a Luo president for the first time in Kenyan history. As voting began and the ballots were still being counted, Kibaki withheld the results that had come in from swing regions. He'd won those regions, although there were serious rumors of voter fraud, and by withholding information, he allowed the hopes and accusations of the Luo constituents to reach a frenzy. At the eleventh hour, he jumped in with the results of the swing votes, won the election (although a Luo might say he stole the election), and paved the way for all hell to break loose throughout the country.

The country was immediately divided, and violence erupted between Luos and Kikuyus. With the police vastly outnumbered, it quickly became a national emergency. Houses and churches were burned with people inside them, machete-wielding men fought each other openly in the streets, businesses shut down, and many participated in widespread looting. There was an automatic assumption that if you were a Luo, you supported one side, and if you were a Kikuyu, you supported the other. Reconciliation between the two sides seemed impossible. But that didn't apply to Cornel and Duncan. They were members of opposing tribes, but they were also best friends whose connection went far deeper than cultural or political divides.

As everyone fled from the major cities to their ancestral homes to find refuge, Cornel and Duncan stayed together in Limuru, which was technically Kikuyu land. Their location meant Cornel was stuck in a high-risk area. It was too dangerous for him and his wife, Irene, who was six months pregnant with their first child, to travel all the way back to Kisumu. Instead, Kim arranged for them to hide inside the Brackenhurst compound, where it was nonpartisan, gated, and safe. They figured they could go home once things settled down. But three months later, they were still there, hiding out in the compound with no option to escape.

Outside the Brackenhurst gates, the rest of the country was still filled with tension, although now of a different kind. As a response to the months of chaos and mass public violence, government systems had shut down, the economy slowed, and people were afraid to go outside. Nobody worked, few had money, and most had no access to daily food rations. The Luo versus Kikuyu brutality morphed into all-tribe agony. Kenyans were now fighting not only because of cultural and political differences but also because they were starving.

Cornel only emerged twice from Brackenhurst in that ninety-day span, once to stealthily drive Irene to the hospital to deliver their baby boy and once to join Duncan in doing relief work.

Right in the thick of the conflict, Cornel and Duncan procured a truck full of food they then drove to areas where the devastation was the worst. Despite the fact that other members of their tribes would interpret a Luo and Kikuyu being seen together as ultimate betrayal, they didn't let it stop them. The two of them traveled around for an entire month, distributing food to those who needed it most, regardless of their tribal affiliation.

They were challenged and threatened by people on multiple occasions, each time forced to explain why they were side by side. They were met with anger, shock, and disgust, and once they were almost killed when Luos with machetes surrounded them and dragged them out of their truck. They stood their ground and reasoned their way out of situations by preaching peace and harmony: "Look at the two of us," Cornel argued. "This is my good friend, and even with all the politics that are going on, he is supporting me and coming with me to help my people. Why would we fight him?"

Through it all, their hearts were bigger than their fear. From the very beginning, their friendship had taught them to challenge the beliefs they had inherited from their closest friends and family members. They found strength in unity with each other. Where public opinion encouraged others under threat of death to embrace segregation, Cornel and Duncan stuck together. They were so bound by their motivation that perception and even imminent danger no longer mattered. It was their will to serve and their solidarity in doing so that allowed them to accomplish more than they ever could have alone. To me, their determination to remain unified in the face of life-threatening adversity was as powerful an act as distributing life-saving food.

Slowly, things in Kenya settled back to normal, in large part because of the UN secretary general Kofi Annan. He flew into the country and led a panel that convinced the two principal parties of the conflict to find a peaceful resolution. After forty-one days of negotiations, they signed a power-sharing agreement where Kibaki remained the elected president and Odinga became the prime minister, a position that had to be reinstated as it had been abolished after Kenya's independence in 1964. A few weeks after the signing, I got a phone call from Cornel and Irene letting me know they were finally home safe with their new son, Justin Annan.

While Cornel was in hiding at Brackenhurst, Duncan had been running what meetings were held at Imani, although they occurred sporadically and weren't highly attended since many had fled the area. Gradually, more and more people returned to the region, and the program got back on track. For Duncan and Cornel, the time away granted them some perspective, and they realized they needed a more definitive structure for the program, especially with the influx of attendees after the transition from the White House to Imani. If they wanted CARE for AIDS to impact people's lives, both in the present and in the future, they needed to think through the progression of the program and establish some parameters. They needed a plan.

I was headed to Kenya for spring break along with one of our board members, Mike Titus, which meant we'd be there in person to attend meetings at the church and help Cornel and Duncan assess where there was room for improvement. It had been about nine months since my first trip, but from the moment I landed in Nairobi, it felt like home. I embraced Duncan and Cornel the same way I'd embrace my own brother (if he'd let me). I was so happy to see them that I could have spent days just catching up. But there wasn't any time to waste. My trip was only one week, and we had work to do. My first order of business was to attend a CARE for AIDS meeting.

Imani Baptist Church was a rectangular building made of corrugated iron sheets that were painted vibrant green. Inside, there were about twenty wooden benches in rows that faced the lectern and rows of windows that allowed for light. It was a Tuesday morning meeting, and the church was packed. The crowd was mostly women, interspersed with a few shy men. Many seemed so fragile that I couldn't believe they'd managed to walk to the church. Everyone seemed transfixed when Cornel and Duncan spoke, as if each word contained the very air they needed to stay alive.

There was an open forum for about thirty minutes when people could share whatever was on their minds—a worry, a new symptom, a prayer request, an example of public judgment—eliciting both tears and praise from everyone in attendance, although the tears flowed the most freely. The attendees were then split into two groups. With one, Cornel discussed a chapter from the book of Job, and with the other, Duncan talked about the different food groups.

Mike and I were so impressed with Duncan and Cornel and with the participation from the crowd. The group seemed to absorb everything. Watching that session, I thought it might only be through releasing their pain that people were able to refill their joy. They looked a little less fragile as they left. Many walked out of the church arm and arm, proving there was more than one kind of support they could seek and find in each other.

Being able to sit in on the meeting gave us the foundation we needed to have some productive conversations over the next few days. Mike and I brought objectivity to the table that Cornel and Duncan didn't have, and we helped them explore different ways they could change things up in order to run the best possible program. We started with the end goal—to transform and empower HIV-positive men and women, both physically and spiritually—and worked backward. What did transformation and empowerment specifically mean? What was currently working, and what was not?

The most obvious difficulty was the sheer number of people who attended the meetings. Because there were so many, Duncan and Cornel weren't able to ensure that individual needs were being met. There wasn't enough time to adequately connect with the participants or devote attention to their specific struggles. Should more meetings be added? Should the meetings last longer? Should the number of attendees be capped? All of these were things we had to consider.

As much as we hated the idea of turning people away, the most practical solution was to limit the number of participants. We unpacked who our ideal participants were and what specific circumstances made them most vulnerable and in need of the program. We made a list of qualifiers, like age range, parental status, and proximity to the meeting location, and thought through a process of recruiting those people into the program.

We talked about the structure of the meeting itself: How could the time be maximized, what things needed to be accomplished for it to be successful, and how many months of meetings would that require? We tossed around ideas like assigning weekly topics to keep the discussion on track, turning counseling sessions into timed one-on-one meetings to increase personal development, and having a preset curriculum to ensure each participant received all the necessary information.

If we did limit the number of participants, we knew we would need to open more meeting centers at more churches. But who could dedicate time to seeking out those churches? How much money was required to open one? How could we accommodate a large number of people in inevitably small churches? We couldn't stand to leave people without a way to take action once again.

By the end of the trip, we were exhausted, but we felt reinvigorated at the same time. Because aspiration was different from implementation, there was a lot still up in the air, but now a plan had begun to take shape. We had at least decided that the time had come for Duncan and Cornel to stop working for Kim and devote their full-time attention to CARE for AIDS.

We'd recently acquired our first US partner church—Dogwood, my home church—and they wanted to sponsor us on a monthly basis. They'd taken up a love offering to kick off the partnership and then pledged their monthly support for us to use as we saw fit. I was humbled by their sacrifice, and I knew they weren't in a position to support causes they didn't wholly believe in. It meant Duncan and Cornel would be able to take a small salary while they continued to grow the program.

When I got home, Zach and I talked at length about the new developments and acknowledged that in order for CARE for AIDS to continue its trajectory, we'd need to make raising money and securing partnerships a priority. Who were we supposed to ask? Where would we find the time to fundraise? We agreed to split the work: I would work on our brand identity, website, and board of directors while Zach put together a ministry brief and started reaching out to American churches with the help of our first two interns, Dave and Steve.

On the Kenyan side, we found that after one church committed, others were more amenable. After Duncan and Cornel had Imani Baptist as a partner, there were other churches that expressed interest, with some eventually reaching out to them instead of the other way around.

I went back to Kenya two more times before the end of that summer. The first was in June with Zach, my dad, and another one of our board members. The second was in August, when I took my mom, Lindsay, a board member, and our two devoted but unpaid interns. That was also the month CARE for AIDS officially opened the second center in Nairobi, which had the first class of eighty carefully selected clients who were enrolled in the newly planned nine-month program.

I went back to school for my senior year at Vanderbilt with everything looking up. Before me sat a full load of credits, at least two more scheduled trips to Kenya, our plan to raise money and awareness for CARE for AIDS, and an impending proposal to Lindsay. All at once, I could see how far we'd come, and how far we still had to go.

# CHAPTER EIGHT

# CORNEL

I remember her phone call as if I received it yesterday. It came after I met Duncan, after traveling to Tanzania and telling him of my burdens under the tree. It came after I started seminary, after I thought I had a plan for my life's work. It came before I met Justin or Irene, before I had children of my own. Yet it had as much importance. That phone call was the event that forever divided my life into after and before. And it came before I was ready to hear it.

I had a mobile phone that was very large, almost the size of a brick. I limited its use to emergencies since I was charged by the minute. Very few people had the number, so when it rang, I knew it was important. Even though June through October is the cool season in Kenya, it did not often rain during those months. On that day when my telephone rang, the rain was falling heavily. I was very concerned about my mother's roof. When I heard her voice on the other end of the line, I thought that was why she called.

"Nang'o wuoda," "Hello, my son."

She did not seem panicked, so I sensed it was not about the roof. Her voice sounded very soft, softer than it had in the recent months, although I had noticed it even then. She spoke barely above a whisper, so my next thought was about my father. Maybe she was hiding from him.

"Has father done something?" I asked her in Luo. She would not admit it to me on that phone call, but he had done something indeed.

She told me he was fine. "Cornel, I am sorry that I have not often called," she said. "You have helped me and supported me, and I am very thankful that you are my son."

Even though I was not her eldest, the responsibility had been placed on me to take care of her and my younger siblings. I did not mind. I only wished I could have done more. At the time of the phone call, I was working casual labor jobs while on break from seminary and ministry. Most of my time over the previous year had been focused on evangelizing and traveling, so I had not made a lot of money to send home to Seka. My mother did not say anything about it. But I knew they suffered without the extra shillings I sent for food and school. There were also recent hospital bills that needed to be paid. Each time I had a break from seminary, I worked very hard to earn as much as I could.

"I have been happy to do that," I told her. "There is more coming."

"I have not called to ask you for money." Her voice sounded louder but forced. "I have called to ask you to look after your brothers and sisters when I am gone."

I opened my mouth to ask where she was going when she said, "I am not going to make it."

There was silence as confusion clouded my thoughts.

Her voice went back to a whisper. "I am battling AIDS."

My mind was full of nothing and everything. My knees collapsed. I fell to the ground. My heart felt separate from my chest. Like it was torn from my body and now struggled to beat on its own. What she said was not true. It could not be true. How?

When? Why? Words did not find me. I tried to say "Mother," but it came out as a sound that could not be recognized.

"I am sorry I have not told you before now," she said.

I focused on my lungs and the breath I needed in order to say, "When?"

"I have known for several months."

I thought back through the last times I saw her. I knew she was not feeling well. It was apparent. She was very cold even when it was warm outside. Two blankets were not enough. Her stomach bothered her. The bottoms of her feet itched. And when she scratched them, they became dark. She had twice gone to the hospital in Kisumu. She told me she only needed to rest.

"You are not going to die," I managed to say. And then, "I am coming."

The tears did not come. Not yet. I was too focused to cry. I got on a *boda boda*, a motorcycle taxi, and directed the driver to my village.

I knew HIV was around me. In my neighbors, in Harrison, in Kisumu. But I did not think it was so close to me. I did not think it was in my family. For the whole drive, more than fifty kilometers, I prayed past the pain in my stomach. It was not the feeling of shame. I did not think of what people would say or what they would think. It was pain for my mother and for how alone she must have felt. The months spent hiding the truth and carrying the burden all on her own.

I rushed inside as soon as I arrived. The home was quiet. I found her asleep in her bed. I was shocked at how thin she had become. The bones in her jaw, her cheeks, and her neck looked like they might come out from the skin. On her arm that was outside of the blanket, I saw many veins. Veins full of poisoned blood.

I did not wish to wake her, so I sat in the doorway of our home and faced outside. I wanted to look out at our land and feel grateful for something. I needed to feel the air. I lowered my head and prayed for breath, for her and for myself. I praised the Lord for our lungs. I praised Him that she was still alive. I prayed that she would wake from her sleep.

After much time passed, she opened her eyes. I moved indoors to sit on the floor next to her bed. She looked surprised to see me, like she did not recall our phone conversation.

She said, "Misawa Cornel, idhi nade?" "Good afternoon, Cornel, how are you doing?"

It was typical of her to focus on anyone but herself. I stroked her hand as a way to tell her I was fine. There was a lot of silence that first day. No words in Luo or Swahili or English could provide what I wanted to say or wanted to ask. She did not seem to have the strength to answer either way. She had not been out of bed for one month. That is what she told me when I was finally able to ask if she wanted to go outside to greet the sun. We both stayed where we were.

My siblings who were still of school age arrived home close to dusk. They said hello to me and my mother and then did their schoolwork. They shared some maize and a banana among them. They seemed very *oyuma*, casual. I knew then that they did not know of her AIDS. They thought our mother was just sickly. Because of her months of decline, they were used to seeing her like that and now did not seem to see her at all. My father did not return home that night, so we did not see him either.

I went back to Kisumu the next morning to report for work. I had secured a three-week job doing demolition at small construction sites. It was steady pay and I needed to honor the commitment, so I had no choice but to leave my mother. I went back and forth each day and spent daylight in Kisumu and evenings in Seka. My mother knew to expect me by late afternoon. Since she could not tell time, she gauged it by when she saw the sun through the gap in the corner of the roof.

For my first few visits, I did not leave her bedside. I held her hands in mine and repeated, "You are not going to die. We are going to fight this now together." I said it both for her and for me. I do not know how much she heard because she was asleep far more than she was awake. As much as I wanted her to rest, I was anxious when her eyes were closed. Her breathing was very slight. Sometimes I could not tell if her chest was rising and falling. I had to hold my breath to become still enough to see her breathing, to see that assurance of life. At least when her eyes were open, I knew she was still with me and that we could both take another breath.

She did not have enough energy for long conversations but would occasionally say small things to me. She apologized for making a *tuomruok*, fuss. She told me she hoped my twin brothers made it through secondary. She asked if it was autumn yet. She said she did not know how she came to die a shameful death.

"There is nothing shameful about you," I whispered. "I love you and support you no matter what. You are not going to die."

I did not know what to do for her. So I prayed. I read to her from the book of Psalms. I told her how God was the one who determined a person's days, not AIDS. I moved her from side to side so one hip was not more painful than the other. I made sure she was warm enough. I did not leave her side unless it was to cry. She did not need to see me be anything but strong for her.

My mother did not have an appetite. But I knew she needed nourishment. She needed to gain strength. With the money I earned from the construction job, I purchased food nearly every day and took it with me to Seka. I bought fish, beans, cabbage, potatoes, kale, and rice from the market. I got fresh milk and eggs from our neighbors. I had one of my sisters show me how to make beef stew and *chapati*, flatbread. I cut up pineapple and passion fruit. I steeped black tea in milk. As the days passed, my mother went from eating only a few bites to what could almost be considered a full meal.

When she ate, I ate alongside her. When she felt too weak to eat, I fed her. When she said she had enough, I distracted her with stories while I raised food to her mouth. I told her about the grounds of Brackenhurst and how I had seen two gray crowned cranes. I told her about my years at IMPACT and the songs I had learned to sing. I told her of my travels and how I went all the way to Mandera in the northeast corner of Kenya. I told her of my new friend, Duncan.

She told me she had married my father when she was thirteen or fourteen. She told me she had long desired to own a dairy cow. She told me her favorite food when she was a young girl had been *githeri*, beans and corn, and today it was *nyama choma*, roasted meat. She told me she got good marks in primary but stopped attending in class 3. She told me the farthest she had traveled was the Kenyan industrial town of Thika.

She began sleeping less and getting out of bed to go to the bathroom. That was a big improvement. And she desired to bathe. Culturally, I could not wash my mother. But I heated water in a pot over the wood fire and then walked her to the *choche maoko*, the outdoor shower. My aunt waited there to help. In less than two weeks' time, my mother began to bathe herself.

When she was finally strong enough to make the trip to the hospital, we boarded a bus together and went to Kisumu. Under a sign that read, *Mapokezi*, Reception, we gave my mother's name and the reason for her visit to a woman who did not look us in the eyes. She pointed toward a door and told us to wait for the doctor on the other side. Through that door was an outdoor area where many others were waiting, maybe thirty others. There were not nearly enough seats, so many lay on the ground because they were too weak to stand. I could barely see the dirt.

Those who surrounded us were very ill. Most looked to be only skin and bones. Some were covered in sores that attracted the buzzing flies. Others had red rashes that looked just as painful

JUSTIN AND HIS DAD AT UHURU PEAK (19,341 FEET)
AT THE SUMMIT OF MT. KILIMANJARO (JULY 2005).

JUSTIN AND HIS DAD AT THE SUMMIT OF KALA PATTER (18,519 FEET) IN THE HIMALAYAS.

# PHOTO ALBUM

BRACKENHURST CONFERENCE CENTER WHERE CORNEL AND DUNCAN
MET ONE ANOTHER AND ALSO MET KIM PACE.

JUSTIN AND ZACH AT THE GLOBAL LEADERSHIP SUMMIT IN AUGUST 2006.

CORNEL AND DUNCAN WITH KIM, JIM, AND MARY PACE.

STUDENT VOLUNTEERS LEADING A TEXTBOOK DRIVE AT FURMAN UNIVERSITY.

OUR FILMMAKING TEAM FOR OUR FIRST TRIP.
FROM LEFT TO RIGHT: JOSH, JON, CORNEL, JUSTIN, DUNCAN, AND ZACH.

JOSH AND ZACH WITH A GROUP OF KIDS DURING OUR DOCUMENTARY TRIP (MAY 2007).

RIDING BIKE TAXIS AROUND KISUMU DURING OUR FIRST TRIP (JUNE 2007).

JUSTIN AND JON RECORDING AN INTERVIEW FOR THE DOCUMENTARY (JUNE 2007).

# PHOTO ALBUM

PAMELA'S HOUSE ISOLATED FROM THE REST OF THE COMMUNITY.

VISITING PAMELA MORE THAN THREE YEARS AFTER OUR FIRST MEETING AND SHORTLY
AFTER HER GRADUATION FROM THE CARE FOR AIDS PROGRAM (DECEMBER 2010).

JUSTIN, LINDSAY, AND NICK IN KENYA SHORTLY AFTER
NICK MOVED TO KENYA (SEPTEMBER 2009).

NICK AND JUSTIN IN THE KARANJEE COMMUNITY–SITE OF THE FIRST CARE FOR AIDS CENTER.

PHOTO ALBUM

OUR FIRST SIX KENYAN TEAM MEMBERS.
FROM LEFT TO RIGHT: KEVIN, CORNEL, ROSEMARY, HUMPHREY, STEVE, AND DUNCAN.

CLIENTS IN OUR FIRST COHORT GATHERING
FOR A SEMINAR AT IMANI BAPTIST
CHURCH (JUNE 2008).

IMANI BAPTIST CHURCH–SITE OF THE
FIRST CARE FOR AIDS CENTER.

CORNEL AND DUNCAN AWARDING THE GRADUATION CERTIFICATE
TO OUR 1,000TH GRADUATE (SEPTEMBER 2011).

ANNE BECOMES THE 5,000TH GRADUATE OF THE CARE FOR AIDS PROGRAM (MARCH 2015).

# PHOTO ALBUM

DUNCAN WITH SIX OF HIS ADOPTED BOYS AROUND 2009.

DUNCAN AND HIS SON, GEORGE, IN 2019.

THE IMPACT MINISTRY TEAM WHERE
CORNEL AND DUNCAN MET IN 2002.

DUNCAN WITH CINDY WILSON, THE
DIRECTOR OF IMPACT AND SPONSOR OF CORNEL
AND DUNCAN'S SEMINARY EDUCATION.

VISITING DUNCAN'S PARENTS IN GITURA.

DUNCAN AND HIS WIFE, ROSE, AND
THREE BIOLOGICAL CHILDREN: KEITH, ABIGAIL, AND ANNAH.

# PHOTO ALBUM

JUSTIN AND HIS FAMILY OUTSIDE OF THE PANCAKE PANTRY IN NASHVILLE.

THE MILLER FAMILY ON CHRISTMAS MORNING 2018.

CORNEL AND DUNCAN ATTENDING AN ATLANTA UNITED SOCCER GAME WITH THE MILLER FAMILY.

JUSTIN'S PARENTS, MARK AND DONNA, WITH HIS BROTHER, DAVID, AT A BASEBALL GAME.

JUSTIN WITH HIS TWO KIDS, ADDIE AND LOGAN.

CORNEL AND HIS FAMILY IN SEKA SHORTLY BEFORE HIS DAD PASSED AWAY (JUNE 2007).

CORNEL AND HIS MOM, NORAH, IN 2018.

CORNEL AND HIS WIFE, IRENE,
AND FIVE KIDS: BRIAN, JUSTIN, SHERRY, COLLINS, AND CORNEL, JR.

CORNEL AND HIS WIFE, IRENE.

CORNEL WITH HIS SON, JUSTIN.

CORNEL, JUSTIN, AND DUNCAN IN 2017 (FROM LEFT TO RIGHT).

as the sores. Very few people were joined by healthy companions. It seemed no one else went with their HIV-positive mothers to the hospital. No husband took his wife. No sister took her brother. It was a lonely disease.

After four hours of waiting, a doctor saw my mother. He verified her status and gave her drugs, or what he called ARVs. She was told to take them every day, once in the morning and once in the evening, and to return to the hospital every month for replenishment. The doctor was pleased to hear about how well she had been eating. He said that, when the medication went into the body, it needed to find something to hold on to.

At first, the effects of the new drugs caused my mother to be very tired and weak. She went back to being in bed during most of the hours of my visits. I read to her from the Gospels, although I started out of order with the book of Luke. Because she did not know the Lord personally, I wanted her to hear the full story, from His birth to ascension. I wanted her to know the struggles He lived through. One day, she asked to know Him and for me to pray with her to find faith. A heaviness released in me that I had not known was there.

I believe my siblings came to suspect how ill our mother was. But they also witnessed the life that came back into her, so perhaps they did not truly believe it was AIDS. I did not know what my father thought as he was not often around. That was not *malich*, abnormal. He had been absent from our lives as much as my mother had been present. As she lay in her bed and struggled to live, there was talk from the neighbors that my father was revisiting the widow who lived up over the hill.

I did not want to be too far away from my mother until I knew she was stable in her health. But she insisted I go. She reminded me of my calling to seminary and said I had given up my life for long enough. I committed to her that I would continue my trips back and forth to Seka, although it would be once every two or three weeks now instead of every day. Limuru was a far journey from Seka.

In the absence of my daily contact with my mother, I wanted to be sure she still felt encouraged to get out of bed. I had come to believe that people died so quickly because they were locked in a small room with nothing but a voice inside them that said AIDS was going to kill them. I wanted to quiet that voice inside my mother and replace it with a reason to rise.

I had saved 7,000 shillings, about US$70, from my demolition work. I gave it to my mother to use as capital to start a fish business. She would be able to go to the market, purchase fish, and then resell them for a profit. It would be a way for her to earn money but also a motivation for her to stay well. Spending a day selling fish at the market could give her something to look forward to, the blessing of purpose.

She was very pleased. On the day I left, she told me what kind of fish she planned to sell and for how much. She said she intended to begin in several weeks' time. I tried to remain unemotional as I thought back to how she was prepared to die only one month before. Her transformation had been a true miracle.

I first rode the bus from Kisumu to Limuru. It was a journey that lasted over eight hours. I spent much of that time in reflection about the past month. And in prayer. I lay my head against the window and spoke to God for hours. I praised Him for His miracles and compassion. I thanked Him for allowing me to bear witness to His power. I asked for His healing hand to continue to touch my mother.

My mind would not clear of all that had passed. I thought about the phone call. The weakness of my mother when I first arrived at her home. The fear that I concealed with hope. The injustice of someone so pure meeting a fate as cruel as AIDS. The nearness of death in the waiting area of the hospital. The worn Bible she asked to keep even though she could not read.

The indifference of my father. The bags of food I left in the corner of the kitchen.

My mother's strength could not be denied. I saw her fight to be strong in all areas. But if she had not had someone step in to guide and encourage her, I do not believe she would have seen past her despair, her submission to death. She may not have realized she was capable of fighting at all. If she had been left by herself, she would have died. Alone in her bed with no food, no one to speak with, no one to pray with, no one to care for her, and no one to give her hope. It was too painful for me to consider.

My heart was heavy for the people who died that way. They suffered alone. Many were dismissed by their loved ones, invisible under the same roof. They were cast aside because the rumors of the disease had disguised who they were apart from their status. Some did not even share the news with their loved ones because their shame was so great. They had no hope for tomorrow. They did not know how to find strength.

I felt anger. It was a feeling of resentment I did not wish to have. I pleaded with the Lord to remove it. I wished to do everything I could to make sure my mother continued to live. But it should not just be my mother. There were other parents in my village who did not have loving families to care for them. They were dying in isolation without anyone offering to understand their *thagruok*, despair. No one was giving them encouragement or hope. And Seka was only a small part on the map. Kenya was a large country. And the continent of Africa larger still. But I was small like Seka. I was only one man. I could not sit with all who suffered. I did not have the means to provide food. I had no formal education to know how to properly counsel those who were infected.

The hopefulness I felt as I left my village was dampened by defeat when I arrived in Limuru. As I walked from the bus station to Brackenhurst, I reminded myself that what mattered most was the improved health of my mother. She had made great strides in a short time. She was alive. She had made a decision of faith. She had a will to live. Those were the victories that I needed to sustain me.

I had long known about the suffering from AIDS. And now I understood. I wanted everyone who suffered to improve like my mother. I wanted them to feel supported. I wanted them to have proper nourishment. I wanted them to feel connected to a loving God. I wanted them to have opportunities to thrive. Who was I to want such things? I thought then of the tree in Tanzania. At least I had one friend who shared my burden. It was *wuoro*, greedy, of me to expect more.

# CHAPTER NINE

# JUSTIN

My senior year at Vanderbilt was well underway by the time Zach and I launched a book drive at Wheaton College. Technically, it was Zach who launched the book drive, as it was his idea and his college. He always had an idea up his sleeve. If he hadn't ended up becoming a pastor, he would have been a serial entrepreneur, and a highly successful one at that.

Zach initially wanted to start a textbook resale business, where he'd buy back books from students and then resell them the next semester at a markup. He amended the direction and told me he wanted to convert that business idea into a fundraising initiative to support CARE for AIDS. I was all for it. I had quickly realized that fundraising was more difficult than I anticipated, and I needed all the help I could get.

The book drive was a genius plan. College students were our people. We knew where to find them and how to talk to them. Since we knew from personal experience that most didn't have any money, we also knew they weren't a viable demographic when it came to traditional fundraising, but they did have textbooks they no longer needed once a semester ended.

At the end of our first semester of senior year, Zach was in Illinois, on the Wheaton campus, collecting books in exchange for T-shirts; that was our trade-off with the students. We'd invested a small amount of money into printing CARE for AIDS T-shirts, and we gave one to every student who donated three books. Through the exchange, we got to spread the word about the AIDS crisis, share with people about the work we were doing, and use the proceeds from reselling their textbooks to help fund our mission.

It was also at the end of that first semester that I asked Lindsay to marry me. I did it on Christmas Day, when she was at home in Fort Worth and she thought I was at home in Atlanta. I'd flown into Dallas–Fort Worth that afternoon and arrived at her parents' house to find her not at home. That evening, when she finally got home, I went back and called her from outside their front door. I told her there was a present waiting outside for her—which was true since I had placed roses on the front step— and she walked out to pick up the bouquet while we were still on the phone. She almost dropped the flowers, and her phone, when I suddenly appeared from around the side of the house and dropped down to one knee. I don't know what I said, but evidently, it was coherent enough for her to know I was proposing marriage. She said yes, which meant that, as we were finishing up our senior year at Vanderbilt together, we were also planning an August wedding.

I remember that season as full in every sense of the word. In addition to going to school, having Ultimate practices four nights a week, competing in tournaments almost every weekend, and helping Lindsay plan our big day, I was orchestrating more book drives with Zach at both Wheaton and Virginia Tech. I looked forward to the funds those would bring in at the end of semester, but in the meantime, I still needed to secure a consistent stream of donations. I knew it was time to focus outside the college box.

Now that there was more substance behind the CARE for AIDS program, I joined Zach in the pursuit of church partners. My dad's favorite saying was "Hope is not a strategy," so I took those words to heart as I headed out like an aspiring mayor on the campaign trail. I did my homework to sort out churches with missions departments that would empathize with our cause or, at the very least, be open to meeting with me. I went armed with CARE for AIDS literature, testimonials from Kenyans in the program, an outline of the curriculum that Duncan and Cornel created, an itemized breakdown of organizational costs, and of course the documentary. Church after church and pastor after pastor closed their doors to the idea—figuratively and, on occasion, literally.

I was discouraged, to say the least. It was baffling to me that more American churches weren't jumping at the chance to support such a remarkable program. It may have been my delivery or my age or the fact that the churches didn't have money to give, but at the time, I only saw an injustice that stunted the growth of CARE for AIDS. Duncan and Cornel put everything they had into expanding the organization, but they were bound by the constraints of the budget.

Hiring staff was our biggest and most immediate need. For each new center we opened, we needed two more counselors—one who focused on health and one on spirituality. Ideally, we'd also hire someone who could manage strategic growth and continue seeking out Kenyan churches to host CARE for AIDS centers. If those churches couldn't accommodate the needs of participants and counselors due to a lack of space, we needed to make an initial investment to create the space ourselves—either through building partitions in the back corners of the sanctuary, where clients could meet with counselors privately, or by constructing counseling rooms from scratch somewhere on the church compound.

Then there was the cost of food. Cornel and Duncan felt very strongly that nutrition was a necessary piece of the model. Much of their health counseling focused on the balance of a proper diet, but it was futile if the clients couldn't afford to purchase the foods they were being encouraged to eat. Cornel and Duncan wanted to supply their clients with one bag of food per week—things like beans, rice, and maize and maybe even seasonal fruits and vegetables.

There were also medical costs associated with caring for people with AIDS. If the clients had an infection or needed surgery, Cornel and Duncan wanted to help offset the cost. If getting to and from the hospital for doctor visits or medication was a struggle, they wanted to ensure that their clients had access to a reliable means of transportation. They wanted badly to eliminate the stress that surrounded the most common roadblocks for clients, and while it was commendable, it wasn't entirely possible—at least not yet.

At the end of a particularly discouraging weekend of meetings with different churches, I was recuperating at my parents' house before heading back to Vanderbilt. I felt sorry for myself, and I wasn't shy about it. I shared my feelings of ineptness with them and then gave them an earful about my frustration with the church. I sounded like Bono at the summit.

"It doesn't have to be someone's fault, you know," my dad said. "Yours or the church's."

Even though I knew he was right, I needed there to be a reason our mission wasn't reaping as much as we were putting into it. So I just stayed quiet.

"What if you're barking up the wrong tree?" he asked.

"What do you mean? What other tree is there?"

"A church is more than the pastor, son."

My mom walked in from the other room and said, "There are plenty of people within the church who might want to be a part of what you're doing."

"You have a board of directors who are supporting CARE for AIDS, and you have friends and family who are too," my dad said. "People care. Just because a pastor says his church won't become a financial partner doesn't mean the individuals in the congregation wouldn't want to give."

My natural preference for structure had clouded my fundraising creativity. For years, my tunnel vision had kept me focused on pastors because they were the ones who approved or denied the church budget. But why had I felt so confined to that idea? From the beginning, Cornel, Duncan, and I always liked the thought of American churches partnering with Kenyan churches, but wasn't it just as commendable to have American individuals helping Kenyan individuals? It was unfair to act like the church as a whole didn't validate CARE for AIDS just because of the dismissal of a missions pastor; maybe the congregation was the key. It occurred to me that I didn't need to place blame. I needed to widen the net.

Like my dad said, there was already support coming in from board members, friends, and family, so Zach and I decided to build momentum and try to increase our individual donor base. We started doing in-home dinners, where we asked current donors and board members to invite their friends. After we all shared a meal, we shared the story of CARE for AIDS, played the documentary, and cast a vision for the ministry. People were receptive. They seemed to like the intimacy of the gathering, where they could get a clear picture of who we were and what we were trying to do. Monthly donations quickly increased enough to allow Cornel and Duncan to move forward with opening another center and hiring the necessary staff.

The next few months leading up to my college graduation were all-consuming. It wasn't just that a lot was going on; it was the imminent knowledge that upon graduation, I'd have some decisions to make about my future. It was the typical wrestling match with identity and purpose that accompanies the onset of real adulthood, enhanced by the realization that I would soon be a married man who also wanted to offer stability to my wife. Was I going to be an official employee at CARE for AIDS? Was higher education my next move? Was corporate America?

My dad started at Chick-fil-A when he was in college, and he was still there decades later. His longevity within the company was something I admired, something I wanted to emulate if I could. I liked the commitment it represented; only he wasn't tied to it for commitment's sake. I watched him put on his suit and Chick-fil-A tie and head into the office every day, and he always seemed genuinely happy to do so. It set a precedent for me that proved it was possible to love your job. I loved the work I was doing with CARE for AIDS, but I didn't know if it was my long-term calling, much less if it could ever sustain a family. I knew I didn't need to decide immediately, but I was often internally consumed by the decision.

Two years earlier, I never imagined CARE for AIDS would be anything but a passion project, but in time, it had turned into a legitimate organization. We'd tapped into something special and had already accomplished a great deal, despite the fact I was only focused on it when I could find the time on nights and weekends. Zach was committed to helping me with book drives for as long as he could, but his plan to pursue a full-time pastoral role after graduation meant it was up to me to double down on my own. There was so much more opportunity we hadn't unpacked yet, and I felt like I owed it to myself, Duncan, Cornel, and the greater mission to commit to it and give it my full attention. I told myself that after a few years, I would appoint a successor, go on to business school, and get a job in the for-profit sector as I had always planned. But for the time being, I'd go all in.

My decision was solidified after some prayer, more conversations with Lindsay and my parents, a handful of job interviews for the sake of testing the waters, and an official submission of my candidacy to the board. When they approved my full-time leadership role, which would take effect on the first of September, I called Cornel and Duncan to tell them personally.

They were ecstatic, although that seemed to be the case every time we spoke. It was apparent to anyone who came in contact with them that they were in their element; they'd found their long-term calling. On practically every phone call we had, they told me how they felt blessed beyond measure. They were so pleased with the state of the program and how well clients were responding to the education, support, and guidance they received at CARE for AIDS. The White House was a busy hub of operations now that more staff had come on board, and the program as a whole was gaining a positive reputation within the community.

By spring, thanks to Dogwood Church, a few dozen individuals, and the earnings from two more book drives, CARE for AIDS had opened a total of three centers, all in churches around the Limuru area of Nairobi. We in no way had deep pockets, but we had enough to cover our needs and still allow for some growth. Cornel and Duncan continued to oversee the health and spiritual counselors and developed our few new staff members. They had a gift for caring for people—clients and staff members alike—and they acted as the keepers of a lot of ideas for how to do that well.

There was one way, in particular, they'd already started implementing every Saturday for kids in the community. They told me about it during one of our biweekly calls, when I questioned a new and recurring charge in the budget.

"It is a need," Duncan said.

"Yes, these are vulnerable children," Cornel added. "They do not have a place to go. Since they are not in school on the weekend and food at home may be sparse, they may go days without being fed. We are starting a program to feed them. We can also teach them about HIV so it will be educational."

I was immediately conflicted. Feeding and caring for Kenyan children was important work—and necessary—but it wasn't exactly in our mission statement. We had just completed months of discussions, including more than a few phone calls with the board, to define our ministry vision, and it was unanimously decided that our focus should be on HIV-positive men and women, on parents. We couldn't afford to divide our attention and take care of kids as well, or we'd go the way of so many other organizations that tried to do it all and inevitably failed.

I ignored the voice inside my head that told me I was a heartless monster who didn't want to feed hungry children, and shared my concerns with Cornel and Duncan—although I was careful not to overplay my role. I wasn't the local, I wasn't the expert, but my job was now to keep the organization on track financially and to offer an outside perspective. I explained that it was a departure from our focus and that we ran the risk of doing too many things, which in turn put us at risk for not doing any of them well.

They understood where I was coming from, and together, we ultimately decided to end the weekend feeding program. It was one of the first tests thrown at our three-person partnership, a definitive example of how it takes actively listening to each other to reach a true consensus. Personal milestones aside, it solidified in their hearts and in mine that our programs were going to be differentiated—that the organization itself was going to be differentiated—based on our ability to focus on one thing and do it really, really well.

Over spring break, Lindsay and my college roommate Nick went with me to Kenya. Lindsay had visited once before, but it was a new adventure for Nick, who finally got to see what had been consuming me for so long. We had a good time staying together at the White House with Duncan, visiting the three working centers, and touring a fourth potential location. It was nice to have Lindsay and Nick there with me, to have people I respected take an interest in something that had become so important to me. Lindsay said she was proud to see how far the organization had come in the six months since she'd last been there, and Nick told me he was impressed with what he'd seen, which meant a lot to me since we'd grown together as peers.

Nick was the top mechanical engineer in our class at Vanderbilt. He was one of those guys who walked into college already having dozens of credits but shrugged it off like it was nothing. His natural state was inquisitive and analytical; that's just how he was wired. He had applied and was expecting to be accepted to a master's program in Australia that started in the fall. When we got back from Kenya, we were all shocked to hear that one of his references hadn't submitted their recommendation on time and his application had consequently been thrown out. He came to me late in the semester and asked, "What do you think about me going to Kenya and helping CARE for AIDS establish some systems and structures to support the expansion of the program?"

I was floored, grateful, and speechless. To say we'd be lucky to have him was an understatement, and I told him so. After a meeting with the board and making a subsequent offer to Nick that would require him to raise his own salary (with the promise of free lodging at the White House with Duncan), it was a done deal.

Soon, it was graduation day at Vanderbilt. It was an exciting day for all the obvious reasons, but for me, it was also a day of reflection. I'd had a bit of an identity crisis after my Ivy League plan didn't pan out, but it turned out that Vanderbilt had been the best place for me all along. I got a wonderful education, met my future wife, and made lifelong friends. It put a different spin on the dream I'd had for my life, which had all started with attending the best college I could. What I'd originally thought was the best wasn't necessarily the best for me. And what I wouldn't have considered the best turned out to be even better. I'd ended up exactly where I needed to be.

For a graduation gift, my dad and I flew to Nepal to climb Mount Everest—a perfect bookend to our Kilimanjaro trek four years earlier. We weren't trying to climb to the top—that was for climbers whose level of expertise far exceeded ours—but set our sights on the south base camp. We both felt very small after we flew into Lukla and looked up from the foot of the Himalayas. It turned out to be a daunting but equally exhilarating experience that was completely different from Kilimanjaro in almost every way. Where Kilimanjaro had different climates, the only climate at Everest was freezing; there was unexpected snow late in the season that made the approach to base camp much harder. We didn't stay in tents but in teahouses along the trail that had flimsy plywood walls separating the sleeping areas. We had Sherpas instead of porters and a far greater ratio of climbers to guide.

The trek lasted about two weeks, and it was filled with icy terrain, high altitude, reflective snow, and hurricane-force winds. The higher we climbed, the more exposed I felt. I was keenly aware of the unknowns that surrounded me—from an avalanche to snow blindness to frostbite. The fact that no matter how much I planned or prepared I ultimately had no control over what lay ahead was evident. It wasn't lost on me how perfect of a metaphor the experience was for my new job, new marriage, and new postcollege life. All of it would be as challenging. As we reached Kala Patthar, the highest point we trekked to, I felt free. Still incredibly vulnerable, but free.

Come August, Lindsay and I got married in Fort Worth and set up house in Atlanta. Cornel and Duncan flew in for the wedding—the first of many stateside trips for them—and Zach, Josh, and Nick stood beside me as three of my groomsmen. Lindsay and I honeymooned in Mexico, and as soon as we got back, I officially joined CARE for AIDS as its sole US-based employee while Nick became the only Kenyan-based employee from the US.

When it came to the CARE for AIDS vision, Duncan and Cornel brought so much heart to the table. They saw the needs of people and understood the ins and outs of what they were struggling with. They immediately had ideas as to how we could help. Unfortunately, heart was only part of the equation; running a business also required structure, reason, and accountancy. We not only needed a why assigned to each idea but also a what. What did that idea really entail? What itemized tasks were associated with it? What were the desired outcomes? What markers were in place to measure its growth? Everything needed to have a rationale behind it and a system around that rationale.

Nick was the perfect person to oversee our operations in Kenya. He worked directly with Duncan and Cornel on the programs and on processes that could make them more consistent and efficient. The three original centers had been launched based on proximity to the White House and the personal relationships Cornel and Duncan had with the local pastors. In his role, Nick began to formulate criteria for future partner churches that would host new CARE for AIDS centers, established appropriate expectations for both parties, and initiated formalized partner contracts.

We began to open centers at a staggering rate—from three to fourteen within the two years that Nick was living in Kenya. It was a blessing in more ways than one because that 350 percent increase translated to over 1,000 HIV-positive men and women being cared for across Kenyan communities. It also meant we provided nearly two dozen Kenyans with jobs as counselors. It felt good to know we were making a tangible difference in so many lives, which I saw firsthand during quarterly trips to Kenya.

Back in the States, I was a one-man show, wearing every hat imaginable. At first, I was energized by the full-time focus on a mission I'd previously only worked on in my spare time.

I was as excited as everyone else about our progress, and I got caught up in it to some degree. I hadn't accounted for the fact that accelerated growth was typically accompanied by growing pains. We'd grown so quickly that cracks in the organization started to show.

Financially, we lost a little momentum by the time we reached that two-year mark with our fourteen centers; funding hadn't kept up with our growth. A huge piece of the problem was on me—as much as I hated to admit it, I wasn't the picture of proficiency when it came to financial management, cash flows, or profit-and-loss statements. I understood it enough to pay the bills and approve expansion using funds I knew we had in our accounts, but that wasn't necessarily the most responsible way to manage everything. Even though it didn't get to the point where I feared we'd have to close our doors, it did get to the point where we were operating on a month-to-month basis.

When I stepped back and looked at my own role, I realized I'd exceeded my own capacity to do all the accounting, administration, and fundraising. I had not built any type of team around me, whether it was volunteer or paid, and aside from Lindsay, I didn't have a support system in the US at all. It wasn't just lonely; it was unmanageable, and I began to think our financial woes were a symptom of my overcommitment.

Nick was feeling the strain too. After two years on the ground in Kenya, he moved back to the US. He committed to staying on with CARE for AIDS for another year, and he became my first stateside team member. He worked out of North Carolina while I was in Atlanta. As a team, we made the decision to halt the opening of any new centers until we could get the organization back into healthy financial standing. Nick alleviated some of my operational duties so I could focus my attention on fundraising, a burden that fell entirely upon my shoulders.

Over the course of the next year, I scheduled meetings, pitched visions, coordinated book drives, applied for grants, and campaigned tirelessly for our cause with individual donors and churches alike. Simultaneously, my indecision about my future resurfaced. It hadn't ever disappeared completely; I'd always held it just below the surface. I had told myself I would devote a few years to CARE for AIDS and then leave to pursue other dreams. A few years came and went quickly, and there I was. How did I feel? Did I still have those other dreams?

Somewhere deep down, I knew these feelings had more to do with the idea of those dreams than the actual dreams themselves. The whole idea of "the best" grad school, job, salary, and life felt less like the customizable adventure I wanted to have and more like the script I had been given or, more accurately, the script I had given myself.

Ever since I was young, I'd been told I had limitless potential. It was meant to be a compliment, a vote of confidence, and it was; in many ways, it gave me wings. But it also became a weight that imposed a subconscious pressure and made me second-guess major decisions. My fear wasn't about failing as much as it was about not reaching my fullest potential. Whether or not I wanted to admit it, I was scared of the perception that nonprofit work was somehow second-rate work, as if the nonprofit sector was for people who couldn't make it in the for-profit world. If I chose that as my permanent path, would I be falling short of my potential?

I was happy in my job. I was overloaded, overpressured, and overcommitted, but I was doing something I was passionate about, something I believed in, something that changed lives in a tangible and permanent way. I needed to take a long, hard look at the balance scale on which my priorities were resting. While I pondered, I studied for the GMAT, just in case.

It was around that time that I went out to lunch with a friend named Eric. We got caught up on each other's lives, and I shared with him my indecision about my future. I told him all the reservations I had—the ideals of my childhood plans, the unsteadiness of the nonprofit world when it came to longevity and pay, the concerns over unmet potential, the uncertainty about grad school. I let it all pour out.

When it came to earning potential, it was less about a certain lifestyle I wanted in terms of houses or cars and more about what experiences I wanted to offer the family that Lindsay and I would eventually have. I saw the value in the things that had shaped me growing up, like quality education, traveling, leadership conferences, climbing mountains, and playing sports. I wanted to afford my family those experiences.

I had already been struggling with the stigma associated with nonprofit work, but there was also the stigma attached to a taboo subject like HIV/AIDS. No one ever said it to me directly, but I assumed that people who didn't know me personally likely thought I was HIV positive. Who in their right mind would make it their life's mission to help people with HIV if they weren't personally affected by it? I'd be choosing a difficult issue as my life's work, a true uphill battle that would only get harder and steeper.

Then there was the dilemma of grad school. I knew I needed to look at the intention behind my desire to attend in the first place. I'd never felt direct pressure from my dad to get my master's degree, but it did feel like an unspoken expectation. He often spoke about his regret over not getting his MBA, so a part of me wanted to remedy that for him. But was that really why I would go? I wasn't opposed to furthering my education, but first, I needed to determine what and whom I was doing it for.

A few days after our lunch, Eric sent me a text, and I read it over and over in the days that followed. It was an honest assessment of how I was clearly striving for something, trying to prove myself, but for what and to whom? He challenged me to find rest in the Lord and to allow Him to prune the areas where I was trying to prove my adequacy.

"His pruning is His protection," Eric wrote.

I look back on that text as a defining moment. What he wrote wasn't new information, but hearing it from a dear friend drove it home. In the days and weeks following that exchange, I slowly began to let go of whatever plans and ambitions I had and handed everything over to God. What did He want for my life? What did He see as my utmost potential? He had placed me in the path of Bono, Kim Pace, Cornel, Duncan, and countless others in Kenya, which ultimately led to the formation of CARE for AIDS. And He had not yet provided a reason for me to veer from that path.

I thought about Colossians 3:23, the verse my dad had quoted to me numerous times over the years, the verse taped inside my high school locker: "Whatever you do, work at it with all your heart as working for the Lord and not for man." As I meditated on it, I began to think about it differently than I had before. It was a verse that, taken by itself, could lead to a lot of striving for the sake of trying to please God. But what if pleasing God was about resting in whom I was, understanding what He created in me, and being a good steward of those things?

I was full of peace when I made the decision to stay at CARE for AIDS long term. As long as God wanted me there, I'd be there. I'd rely on the compassion, leadership, and initiative that He created in me and use it to serve our clients and team.

It turned out to be one of the best decisions I'd ever make.

# CHAPTER TEN

# DUNCAN

I can remember many moments that changed the direction of my life completely. When I became sick, it caused me to become a better student. When my father forgave me for being sneaky, it caused me to want to follow his footsteps into ministry. When I began to work with Cornel, it caused me to care for those I did not understand. And when I adopted George, it caused me to put my love for him above all else.

When I brought George home from the slum in Huruma, I lived with Cornel outside of Brackenhurst in a small home of only one room. It was in the nearby town of Ruaka, in a neighborhood called Banana Hill. Fortunately, it was not a lot of money, and we shared everything within our tiny home except for our beds, which was good because all of a sudden I had to share mine with George. Living in one room made it easy to watch George when I was home with him. Because he was used to surviving on his own and scavenging for food, he was always curious about things. It was a relief when he could play with the children of our neighbors, who took care of him every time Cornel and I left for ministry. For two months, I stayed with him in the home when I could and left him with the neighbors when I could not.

Since I was still in seminary and involved in missions, sometimes my work meant going a great distance away from Ruaka and staying somewhere for weeks before I came back. Then I was just twenty-four years old, I was single, and I realized it would be too hard for me to stay with him at home. I decided the best thing would be to take him to a boarding school where I knew he would be safe. Cornel was envious when I told him. It was his dream as a boy to go to boarding school. I found one school near the home of my parents in Nakuru. I knew the teachers there, and I knew my parents were close if anything were to happen. The principal told me about the calendar for that school and how George would be there for three months, then he would come home for one month, and then he would go back to school for three months. To me, that was the best solution. They took children as early as five and six, so I enrolled George in class 1 and committed to paying. It was not a lot of money, but then I did not have much to spare. I began to do manual work to find some money to pay for the school fees. I was happy to do it because it was for my son.

One day, when George was in class 2, I received a call from the school. I did not know then that it would be one of those moments that changed my life. I was in Kampala, Uganda, for a mission with an American team when the principal called me on my mobile phone. I had purchased the phone, the size and color of an African gray parrot, so that they could reach me if there was an emergency with George. I did not use it for anything else, and the ringing alone surprised me. I was immediately worried something had happened to my son.

"Hello, Duncan. This is Jacob, the principal from George's school." First, my heart stopped, and then it started beating faster than I could count. "George is fine, but we want to talk with you. Are you available to come to the school?"

"No," I said to Jacob. "I am in Uganda. Did he do something wrong?" If he was fine, then it must be something else. Maybe he got into trouble. Somehow it made me feel better to know he was not hurt. He was only sneaky like I was at his age, and the thought made me smile.

"No, he did nothing wrong," he said. "But we want to see you in school tomorrow. Can you please come to meet with us?"

My smile disappeared. Even though I told him again that I was far away, Jacob insisted I come, so I knew it must be serious. I took a night bus from Kampala all the way to Nakuru, near my home village, and the following day, I was in the school.

I went to the office to meet with the principal. Still, my heart was beating twice as fast, once for me and once for George. When I sat down, Jacob told me that George was not moving forward. He said they tried everything. For two years, they had been teaching him and feeding him, but he was not changing. Physically, my son was not growing, he was still the same size as he was on the day he first attended, and he was not making friends either. He was a nice boy, Jacob said, but he seemed stressed. He was always quiet, all by himself, and he did not like to socialize. I cannot say that I blamed George. Even though he had had brothers and sisters, he spent many years on his own, without others to show him friendliness. Although I had explained this to Jacob when I enrolled George, I told him again about where my son came from. I reminded him that George was living as an orphan in a slum when I found him. Still, Jacob insisted I take the boy home. He said the boarding school was not doing my son any good and that their environment was not the best place for him. Instead, I should take him home, where I could see for myself how he was doing every day.

At the end of the meeting, they gave me no choice. Already, they had packed his belongings in a box, and they made me sign that I was taking him from school. As we left, Jacob stopped me at the door and stood close to me. In a much quieter voice than before, he said that I should seek counseling from a medical doctor because they believed George had a condition. He gave me a letter and suggested a doctor who could help me understand what was wrong with my son. I did not like that thought, that there was something wrong with my son. To me, he was perfect. I loved him from the moment I brought him home. It was as though we had traded roles from the time I first saw George. In this situation, I was feeling like Laura, the American woman who only saw a boy in need, and the school was feeling like I once did, hesitant to believe anything could be done for the boy.

I did not understand what they were talking about, but I thought they must know more than me, so I did exactly what they told me and took George to the hospital. It was called Kijabe, one of the most respected mission hospitals in Kenya, and I presented the letter to a doctor. I explained everything that happened at the school, and he said he wanted to do some tests. It did not give me any comfort that the doctor was also not sure what could be wrong.

The hospital grounds seemed almost as big as Brackenhurst. There were rooms for patients and rooms for surgery. There was grass in between the buildings and trees all around. I walked back and forth while the doctor did the tests and then he called me into another room. I did not know if he had the answers, but the doctor asked many questions. He wanted to know where I grew up, where I met George, and where we lived together. Then he asked if I knew anything about AIDS. I knew about it, yes, but I did not know what that had to do with my son. At first, I prayed he would just tell me, and then I wished I had not prayed at all because it was then that the doctor looked at my eyes and said to me, "Duncan, did you know that this boy lives with HIV?"

My head felt light, and my legs felt heavy at the same time. I heard it, but I could not process it. All this time, I felt called to help those who suffered with this disease, and I had not known it was in my own son? I had many more questions at once. How did this happen? Where did it come from? What did it mean? What was I to do? Then I became afraid for myself. Did I have HIV? I had been with George for two years, and I never knew, and we shared everything. The home we lived in, the bed we slept in, the food we ate with our hands. I thought to myself, I cannot get this. I did nothing wrong.

I was immediately ashamed of my thought. Those were the words of my father, not my own. He had believed it was a sinful disease and a punishment from God. People with AIDS were sinful, he thought, and that was why those things happened to them, that was why they were dying. What would my father say now? How would he treat us? During breaks from boarding school, George sometimes stayed with my parents if I was on a long-term mission. Would my father be angry that he had allowed a boy with HIV into the home?

In my life, I had already seen him turn away from people he knew very well. I remembered a time when we were walking home together from church and we saw a man who was a good friend of his. When I pointed to him so we could say hello, my father crossed the street without looking up. He whispered to me, "Mukingo." He did not want to be so close to someone who might have weak neck, even if it was someone he had once called brother. That was the behavior of my father in my youth. And it was not just him. It was many others in my village. People in the community rejected those with HIV. They were never invited for anything, their children were not allowed to play with other children, and neighbors would not show up to their homes. They were lepers who suffered by themselves until they died. Even though years had passed and many had come to understand truths about the disease, all those things were still in my head, and they came one by one so that I did not know what to think anymore.

At first, I refused when the doctor asked if I wanted to take an HIV test. I could not stand to think of what would happen if it came back positive. More than once, he said that I should, if only for the boy. He assured me it was better for us both if I knew, and he was right.

I was relieved when the test returned negative. They told me I was clean, and I thanked God. That meant I would still be able to care for George, who needed me even more now than ever before. Still, it was not easy to overcome the shock. Even if I would be okay to have a son with HIV, how would our community receive him? How would our friends, family, and neighbors react once I took him home? I prayed they would not be hesitant to accept him. I did not want him to feel judged. He needed only to focus on getting better, not on fighting off their shame. He needed all of his strength to get well. That was when I remembered how serious a disease it was and how afraid I felt. What if he did not get well? What if he got sicklier? What if he was hospitalized? What if my son died?

"Duncan, this is a walking miracle." That was what the doctor said that woke me from the cursed images I saw. He said he believed that George was born with the virus and that it was likely what his parents died from and why he was left alone in the Huruma slum.

This boy, my boy, survived to seven years with the virus, with no medication, with no care, with hardly any food, with nobody knowing. Many children did not survive more than a year or two without care. But not George. He was still there. At that moment, my love for him grew even bigger. I looked at the doctor, but I did not cry, and I did not smile. I just listened. I knew that was my moment, my moment to recommit myself to my son. I knew the whole world might run away from him, and I would be the only one around, just like when I found him. I had grown so much since then, the Lord had readied me for this moment, and now

I could practice even more love and offer more compassion and protection for George. Because he was my miracle.

That is what I told my father when I arrived at the home of my parents. I took George there after we left the hospital because it was close and we were both tired from a long day. I sat with my father right away because I could not bring my son inside before I told him what happened. I could not ask him to welcome someone inside who had HIV if he did not know first. That would be like asking him to put himself through all the shameful thoughts I had just experienced myself. My father, who had grown close to George over our years together, said nothing at first. In his silence, I recalled when I shared with him the information the government had released about HIV. I did that a year before as a way to prepare him for what I felt called to do after seminary. I knew he would not like the idea of me working with people who suffered from HIV unless he was more educated about it. And even though he never confirmed it to me, I believed my father read the information. I believed he knew that people who were infected did not deserve their fate. I believed that he would never place judgment upon a child for having contracted it. I had to believe it.

My father spent three days away from us before he came back home, and when he returned, he still said nothing. He only lifted George from the dirt floor and hugged him tight.

When George and I finally went home, I asked him to play outside while I spoke to Cornel. There were no other children around, so I did not yet need to concern myself with sharing the news with my neighbors. I cleared my thoughts and poured two cups of tea while I explained to Cornel why I had been called home from my mission in Uganda so soon. I told him about the school and the doctor, and when he asked what they found, I told him what I could not imagine. My son had HIV.

I was surprised that when I shared with him about George, he was not shocked like I was. Instead, he reminded me of a conversation we had years before. He asked me to recall the day he shared with me about Norah, his mother.

"Duncan, do you see?" Cornel said as he set down his tea. "The Lord was preparing me then in order to help you now."

He reached across our small table and grabbed on to my shoulder.

"What you feel about George I felt about my mother. The confusion and the worry and the pain, I felt it."

I looked into the eyes of my friend, who had become closer than my brother. He knew. He knew how I felt that day and how I would feel the next day and all the days that followed. He knew what I would struggle with while I cared for George. He knew what George would struggle with and how hard his life would be. He knew because he had already come out the other side.

Cornel could see that the last few days had been hard on me. Me more than George, who was aware of his illness but did not yet understand its importance. I understood for both of us, and I had not been sleeping well or eating very often. I was very distracted and very weary. I found some solace when I spoke to the Lord, but it was hard to keep my worried thoughts out of my prayers. Cornel saw me and knew.

"You should rest," he said.

"George is the one who needs to rest."

"Celebrate his good days. Do not treat him as a patient until he is one."

I sat with my tea as I listened to George kick the football out-side, the one we had made together out of sisal leaves and rope. That was the first day he called me his father. "Dad Duncan" is what he said.

I thought then of his birth father, his birth mother. They had been infected and then passed it on to sweet George when he was born. I could not imagine my life without George, and did not ever want to, but I knew that his parents should have been the ones to be there with him. Every child deserved the joy of being raised by the people who the Lord entrusted to deliver them.

I thought of the circumstances of his parents, how it was likely that no one in their community did anything to help them when they fell ill. Maybe they were not even welcomed into church. If they had been taken care of or supported, maybe they would be alive to see their son play with his football. If they had somebody like Cornel who saw them and knew them and stood with them, maybe they would not have been forced to turn their children into orphans.

I did not want that to happen to anyone else. I did not want to see other children who had sick parents become orphans. Cornel had not wanted that to happen to his siblings. Together, we did not want anyone we knew in the village who did not have loving families to suffer alone any longer. We wanted all of them to continue to live and to have people to care for them. Over our cups of tea, we knew that we needed to be those people. We had already felt that calling, but it was clear now more than ever that all of this was the work of God. In the situation with his mother and the situation with George, we were being prepared. But first, I had to make it through.

For weeks and months, the things I feared would happen began to happen. I shared the news about George with some trusted friends, and they stopped visiting. The neighbors I used to leave George with no longer accepted my requests to watch him when I traveled. I struggled to find schools that would accept him after I was honest about his HIV status. I realized how HIV was not only isolating for the person who was infected but also for the people who loved them.

George's health went through times of bad and good. One day, he was well, but the next, there were sores on his body. I found a day school that accepted his enrollment, but then his sight gave him trouble and he could not read the textbooks. I was very strict with his diet after learning from Cornel the importance of balance, but then his stomach did not want to hold more than bananas and water. He went in and out of the hospital and was given different kinds of medication. He was always a happy boy, even when he was weak and he could not manage to open his eyes.

He slowly learned how to live with HIV, and I slowly learned how best to support him. Sometimes I cleaned his sores or put drops in his eyes, and other times I just sat with him so he knew someone was there. Each day that passed, my heart grew for George and for the people I had yet to meet who would need the same type of care. I took it as a sign that the Lord was developing in me a strength I could give to those who had been made weak. I knew this journey would one day help me serve my greatest purpose.

# CHAPTER ELEVEN

# JUSTIN

I lifted my arm to knock, and this time, Cornel didn't stop me. It was the same small house with a pitched roof made of metal sheets, but the windows weren't boarded, and the air around the home felt lighter than I remembered, the swamp less swampy, and that palpable isolation was now punctured with other homes built up around the area. Seconds after my knock, Pamela threw open the door and swept me in through the threshold into her home. She hugged me with so much strength I had to catch my breath—this neck-breaking hug from a woman I had feared would wilt from the effort of speaking the last time I saw her. Cornel and I had gone to visit Pamela again about three and a half years after my first trip to Kenya. She was still a small woman, but her warmth filled the room and burst out through the windows and open door.

I had expected to find a healed woman, but Pamela's transformation hit me in ways I didn't expect. From the moment I heard the report from Cornel that she had joined the CARE for AIDS center at one of our partner churches in Kisumu, I knew I would make the journey to visit her again one day. What I didn't know was how deeply the visit would impact me. Pamela had graduated from the nine-month program and had experienced drastic changes in her physical health, as I had anticipated. The wounds that covered her skin five years earlier had all healed, and her scars were smooth and beautiful—a testament to long suffering and the texture that comes from a life of hurt and healing. She no longer walked with a body full of sadness but bounded around her home, creating space for Cornel and me to sit and enjoy refreshments with her. Her eyes closed, not out of pain or shame but out of contentment when she talked about her journey and savored her steaming tea. No, the physical changes didn't surprise me (although they thrilled me). It was the change in her spirit that struck me. In the course of the program, Pamela reconciled with her family. When I had visited five years earlier, I hadn't even realized she had children, but she had regained custody, and they were all she could talk about during this visit. Her parents were back in her life, and although she still had a one-room house, it was a house full of furniture and cooking supplies and toys. A house with light streaming through the wide-open windows. A house so full of hope you could taste it. The difference in her life was astounding, and it filled me with an emotion that is still hard to name—a dizzying combination of pride and humility. Cornel was surely feeling the same thing. He chatted with her in Luo and could barely keep up in translating for me between their fits of laughter. The program worked; Pamela was the literal living proof. I had never felt more resolute about our decisions and the journey that led us to that moment.

In the years between the first class of clients at Imani Baptist and that trip to visit Pamela, CARE for AIDS had grown tremendously. Nick's time in Kenya was marked by growth and streamlining as he built out necessary infrastructure within the program and organizational structure. Cornel and Duncan transitioned from being center counselors to country directors, and we expanded our operations across four regions in Kenya. We had traded in much of our old college-try spirit for a more mature, holistic approach to running an organization, and the effects were transformational for both the clients and the staff.

The way we saw it, if we wanted to truly change lives, we would have to make sure clients' recovery was holistic. If total life change was what we were after, we had to empower our clients from every angle. We originally established physical and spiritual health as the two main pillars of the program, but we soon decided to expand our attention to address economic, social, and emotional transformation as well.

The need for economic support stemmed from Cornel's idea to set his mother up with a fish business at the onset of her recovery. That small business got her out of bed by giving her something to look forward to each day, but it also provided her with some extra money, which was a relief for someone who would consistently face the unexpected costs that came with ongoing care. Many of our clients found themselves in dire financial situations. Some were fired from their jobs after their HIV status was discovered, some were cut off from their spouses when they got kicked out of the home, and some felt they had no skills that would make them employable in the first place. No matter which scenario they found themselves in—in many cases, all were applicable—each one of them could benefit from taking control of their livelihoods. To provide that empowerment, each center started hosting twice-monthly seminars around financial literacy and practical skills that fit local markets, like soap making, beadwork, peanut butter making, and candle making.

Comparatively speaking, the need for emotional support was less obvious. Our health and spiritual counselors already spent a good amount of one-on-one time with the clients, which we took to mean that the clients were feeling heard and that their emotional needs were being met. And as it pertained to physical health and spirituality, they were. To ensure that the clients had an outlet for all the thoughts and feelings they were processing that fell outside of those boxes, our counselors began doing home visits as well—another program component inspired by Cornel's experience with his mom. The visits were a time for open discussion in the comfort and familiarity of the clients' own homes. Sometimes it lent space to multiple voices, since the clients could invite friends or family to attend if they wanted, and sometimes the visits were filled with silence that simply served the purpose of making a client feel worthy of visitors. Either way, it helped address the issue of self-stigma and promote a healthy expression of dignity and self-worth. We also added an official group therapy component to the program to guard against the clients feeling too isolated. Group therapy bolstered the social support that the clients found in one-on-one counseling, and it made space for deep friendships to form that lasted long beyond graduation.

We implemented all five focus areas into the program curriculum—physical, spiritual, economic, emotional, and social—and rolled it out at each of the centers. To ensure our effectiveness, we created a monitoring and evaluation team to conduct interviews with clients at program intake, program exit, and one year after graduation. That accountability set a new standard for us and drove our thirst for impact.

Steady growth and positive impact weren't limited to CARE for AIDS as an entity; they extended to Cornel and Duncan's influence in the community as well. After they shifted into directorial roles and started overseeing the day-to-day operations of all the centers throughout the region, Cornel's focus slowly found its way to organizational culture. His approachability and empathy made him the go-to person for staff members; they gravitated to him to discuss anything from concerns to wins, and he became the champion of staff culture. Over the years, he stayed at the helm of staff development, traveled to different regions to lead listening sessions, and kept a pulse on the health and happiness of all team members to ensure they were thriving. During election seasons, he led additional staff discussions to make sure everyone felt safe and comfortable despite their various tribal backgrounds and political affiliations.

Cornel's influence continued to extend far outside the walls of CARE for AIDS: He sat on the board of directors for his former high school, as well as for Blue Sky Adventures, formerly Brackenhurst Adventures, which Kim Pace had started. He joined the pastoral team at church, got involved in the mentorship of university leaders, and did what he could to support over half a dozen young people by paying for their school fees and upkeep. His ravenous desire for education as a child grew in him an empathy unparalleled in anyone I've met. Even though he's currently in a PhD program, that's the last thing he will tell you in an introduction. He's much more likely to talk about his family, our clients, and how passionate he is about affording everyone the opportunity to learn and thrive.

His mother's health continued to improve, and her viral load—the amount of HIV genetic material found in the blood—had remained at an undetectable level ever since Cornel intervened. She became an unstoppable force in her village, even more so because of the courage and self-assuredness it took for her to disclose her HIV status to family and friends. She kept up with her fish business, had limitless energy when looking after her grandchildren, and continues to inspire clients and donors with her testimony.

Alongside Cornel, Duncan's role of country director at CARE for AIDS evolved as a result of his gift for being good at details and even better at navigating many of them at once. He began to oversee the many moving parts of program operations, which included supervising all regional coordinators and department directors, ensuring that the right church partnerships were being fostered, keeping everything on schedule, and tracking the program's impact on clients. He could be everywhere at once, and as a result, he became well known and well connected in the community, both on behalf of CARE for AIDS and in his own right. He joined the board of directors for his childhood school district, was single-handedly responsible for bringing electricity and a community borehole to his village, and started multiple side businesses he handed over to his family members as a way to ensure their income.

In 2011, Duncan met and married Rose. They started a family and had twins—a boy and a girl—before welcoming another daughter two years later. His three biological children filled a home alongside their older brother, George, as well as a whole slew of foster brothers Duncan began taking in prior to marrying Rose.

Duncan's heart was always set on orphan prevention, which guided the objectives of CARE for AIDS. He committed to steering the organization toward caring for HIV-positive parents before their situation became dire, but he also wanted to step in and do something about the orphan crisis for kids like George who had already lost their parents, to help grow and shape the character of young boys and to enable them to be the men that God intended them to be.

About two years after he adopted George, Duncan went to the Ministry of Gender and Social Services to see what else he could do to support more orphans. Because he was still single and didn't have the financial status that would allow him to properly care for a large group of boys, he was advised to start a foster home; the government would then legally allow him to house the children and employ somebody who could take care of them.

So that's exactly what he did. At first, there were three boys, then seven, then fourteen, totaling close to thirty over the years. Duncan's belief that it was better to build boys than mend men—a nod to a WinShape idea Chick-fil-A's founder Truett Cathy had shared with him—never wavered. As his devotion grew, he began building a boys' center that could accommodate over three dozen children at a time. It wasn't just somewhere for them to live but also a safe and healthy environment where they could connect with one another, focus on schoolwork, and learn vocational skills; it wasn't just about their present but about their future too. Duncan's dream of being a pastor like his dad came true, but the walls of Duncan's church are the walls of a foster home, which he never could have expected.

Eventually, George joined the ranks of his father, living onsite and helping to run the foster home Duncan had started. Despite enduring a decade of health struggles, George completed both primary and secondary school. After he'd reached viral suppression for a number of years, he was asked to become a peer mentor at an AIDS clinic for children, a job he loved because it provided him with a deep sense of purpose. Through that opportunity, he was offered a full-time job at Nazareth Hospital to work with families whose children were HIV positive. His role allowed him to walk with families as they navigated the repercussions of their loved ones' disease, paying forward his gratitude for a life he calls "luckily blessed."

There was no shortage of blessings back in the States either. I eventually went to grad school and got my MBA—two years after Eric's text, after I went all in with CARE for AIDS, and after waiting until the desire was based in God's calling, not my own ambition. At the age of twenty-seven, and with Lindsay carrying our first child, I enrolled at Emory's Goizueta Business School and took night classes across a multitude of concentrations like organizational management, marketing, managerial accounting, and social enterprise. I learned a great deal that I was able to apply to our model, our client services, and our donor communications. Through it all, though, I have still learned the most from my trips to Kenya.

I have had the privilege of traveling to Kenya more times than I can recall, and I always try and orient my trips around attending a CARE for AIDS center graduation. Each one feels momentous, even after going to dozens. There's significance to watching clients receive their physical certificate, as if they're declaring their strength and commitment to their own health as soon as they hold it in their hands. Graduation feels almost sacred. When I see clients walk—or, more accurately, dance—down the graduation aisle, it feels like my past, present, and future collide. Through these graduates, I see where I've been, where I am, and where I am headed. CARE for AIDS was the catalyst that made the metamorphosis possible, for them and for me.

I can clearly see that the most fortunate people don't have the greatest wealth, the loudest voice, or the most knowledge. Instead, the best humans value empathy—deeply understanding other people's hopes and needs—above all else. I have been privileged to stand beside empathetic people my whole life—David, my parents, Cornel and Duncan, the many mentors who acted as guideposts along my unconventional path—and that list, of course, includes Zach, Nick, and Josh. Even as my childhood friends decided to pursue their own dreams, we remained close friends, bound by the experiences we shared, the challenges we faced, and the milestones we accomplished. In their own ways, they all continue to support CARE for AIDS. I am forever grateful to the forces that brought us together all those years ago.

Our team at CARE for AIDS wouldn't have found each other if it weren't for Kim Pace, who was my first connection to Kenya and introduced me to some of the most important relationships of my life. As she continued to travel back and forth between Kenya and the States to run her team-building ministry, she remained a constant fixture in Nairobi, as well as in the lives of Cornel, Duncan, and me. In January of 2018, she was in a paragliding accident while riding tandem with an expert in the

Kerio Valley in western Kenya. Both she and the pilot tragically lost their lives.

The shock and devastation over her sudden death made us feel hollow, as I'm sure it did countless others around the world who were touched by her life and ministry. Her passing was bittersweet; we knew where she'd gone, which in fact made her the lucky one, but we mourned the loss of her earthly presence. I attended her memorial service in Georgia while Duncan and Cornel attended the one held in Nairobi; both were standing room only. Even in death, she brought people together.

Kim was a fundamental piece of the creation and progression of CARE for AIDS. She was the connector who introduced me to Cornel and Duncan, the giver who offered up her home and contacts during my first trip, and the mentor who guided us through the unknowns of starting an organization in Kenya. She was a consistent and inspiring friend whose appearance in our lives topped the list of extraordinary circumstances that propelled our journey forward. A journey that, against all odds, catalyzed a church-based response to HIV that has changed tens of thousands of lives.

Being on the front lines of how African and American churches have responded to the AIDS crisis has also been a lesson in patience and aspiration; in both cases, the headway has been slow but promising. CARE for AIDS still hikes a daily hill riddled with stigma and misgivings about AIDS, and the placement of compassionate and enlightened churches has been imperative in staying the course and growing our number of centers—whether those churches have been overseas partners or faithful stewards of resources here in the US. What I learned after I reframed my reliance on the church as an entity and instead sought individual congregants still holds true today: CARE for AIDS is for people, by people; it is not driven by institutions but by the individuals who uphold them.

Years ago, when CARE for AIDS was just a subtle nudge in our gut, we were all young men in the middle of a transition, searching for our life's purpose, and striving to better ourselves—through education, achievement, success. It wasn't until we came together that our efforts culminated to achieve something that extended beyond ourselves. It wasn't easy; Cornel, Duncan, and I come from such different places. Our nationalities, traditions, education, affluence, and leadership styles were distinct in every discernible way. Cornel is from the Luo tribe, Duncan is Kikuyu, and I am mzungu—a white person in Kenya. Tribal boundaries alone make it inconceivable that we would come to know each other, let alone be as close as brothers. We were raised in different corners of the world with different influences, levels of faith, hardships, and opportunities. Yet the relationships we formed became proof that the most beautiful, fruitful, and restorative relationships are with people whose lives are so different than our own. It's through embracing the differences—embracing them with the neck-breaking strength of Pamela's hug that day—that we finally come to see the similarities.

We are a testament to the fact that we can all participate in the work of restoration and reconciliation if we are willing to get close to people and problems that make us uncomfortable. We need only to acknowledge that there is inherent value in all human life, that the things that unite us go far beyond blood.

# ABOUT CARE FOR AIDS

CARE for AIDS currently operates centers in over sixty communities throughout East Africa (Kenya, Tanzania, and Uganda), and each center is located within a local church. This model is local, cost effective, and discreet for clients. Each center has two local African counselors who guide 80 HIV-positive clients through a nine-month process. Throughout the nine months counselors work to empower clients in five main areas: spiritually, physically, emotionally, socially, and economically.

Cornel, Duncan, and Justin still serve as the leadership team of CARE for AIDS. The hundreds of African staff members have served over 15,000 adults living with HIV, and those graduates represent nearly 50,000 children who are no longer at risk of being orphaned by the AIDS epidemic.

CARE for AIDS has committed to empowering 100,000 people living with HIV by the end of 2027. To learn more about the organization, visit www.careforaids.org.

# ABOUT THE AUTHORS

**DUNCAN KIMANI KAMAU** grew up on a coffee farm in Central Kenya. As the son of a pastor, Duncan grew up with a heart for compassion and pastoral care, which eventually led him to engage in the AIDS crisis by activating local churches to care for the most marginalized members of their communities. Duncan serves as a Co-Founder and East African Director of CARE for AIDS in Nairobi, Kenya, where he and his wife, Rose, live with their three biological children—Keith, Abigail, and Annah—and seven adopted boys.

**JUSTIN T. MILLER** grew up in Fayetteville, GA, and has spent the past decade working to solve some of the world's most complex social problems with the heart of an entrepreneur. As the Co-Founder and CEO of CARE for AIDS, he has dedicated his life and leadership to empowering people throughout East Africa to live a life beyond AIDS. Justin's home base is Atlanta, GA, where he leads the US office of CARE for AIDS. Justin and his wife, Lindsay, have two beautiful children—Addie and Logan—and one on the way.

**CORNEL ONYANGO NYAYWERA** is a pastor, husband, and father. He serves as East African Director for CARE for AIDS, a nonprofit he co-founded in 2007. Cornel grew up in Western Kenya near Lake Victoria, where his passion for justice and inclusivity led him to engage in the HIV crisis that was destroying his community. Cornel and his wife, Irene, now live and serve in Nairobi, Kenya. They have five children—Brian, Justin, Sherry, Collins, and Cornel, Jr.

# ACKNOWLEDGMENTS

### DUNCAN'S ACKNOWLEDGMENTS

Let me start by thanking my wife, Rose, and my children, Keith, Abigail, and Annah, who continue to inspire me and are the reason I wake up every day. The challenges we have gone through and the persistence Rose has shown have proven to me that she was the only one for me. You have always been a loving and caring wife and mother to our kids. I sincerely appreciate you, my dear.

My parents, Rev. George and Mary, deserve so much gratitude for patiently raising me despite my childhood antics. When people will ask me which college I went to, I'll say, "It doesn't matter because it is my parents who made me what I am today." Thanks for introducing me to the greatest teacher—Jesus Christ. Love you.

Cindy and Keith Wilson, thank you for believing in me and giving me the opportunity to serve at IMPACT. You modeled servant leadership so well, and your example still influences my leadership to this day.

A very special thanks to my adopted son, George. I never expected to be adopting a son as a single twenty-four-year-old, but it would be one of the greatest blessings of my life. I count it as a privilege to be your dad, and your courage in the face of HIV inspires me. Thanks for helping me discover my passion to strengthen families and prevent children from becoming orphans.

## JUSTIN'S ACKNOWLEDGMENTS

I must start with my esteemed co-authors and co-founders. They have guided me on this tremendous adventure these past twelve years. I've experienced and learned more than I could have hoped for in a lifetime. Cornel and Duncan, thanks for believing in and putting up with a nineteen-year-old mzungu.

My wife, Lindsay, is the strongest person I know, and she is intricately woven into every detail of this story. I would not have the courage or capacity to do this work without her constant encouragement and support. She deserves as much praise for any success that I have in my life. Baby, you have made endless sacrifices for me and CARE for AIDS, and I can never fully express my gratitude. I love you!

To my kids, Addie, Logan, and the one on the way, you three make me a better man every day. From your childlike faith and your hysterical wit to your unbridled joy and your unselfish love, you teach me more than you know. I hope you will see that I am always faithful to God, your mom, the three of you, and the call that God has placed on my life.

My parents, Mark and Donna, are my heroes. They gave me every opportunity and cultivated in me this wild idea that I could accomplish anything I wanted to, but obedience to God's call was paramount. They have supported me in starting CARE for AIDS from day one, and as an author himself, my dad has been my biggest champion for writing this book. Mom and Dad, thanks for setting an example in faith, marriage, parenting, vocation, and more. I want to be like you when I grow up!

To my brother, David, you are my inspiration. Without ever saying a word, you have brought out the best in me and the people around you. I thank God that He gave me you as a brother.

Each person only finds a handful of lifelong friends, and I couldn't ask for any two better than Josh and Zach, my other

CARE for AIDS co-founders. Zach, I wouldn't have ever gotten on a plane to Kenya without your prodding and to think of the adventure I would have missed.

I can't forget my grandparents, Marion and Beverly White and Tommy (Pop) and Avis Miller. They set in motion a legacy of faith that continues today. Pop, I wish you were here to see this book. You would have been our proudest supporter. A special thanks to Nick Gordon for his unmistakable impact on my life. From our college dorm room in Nashville to Nairobi, his fingerprints are all over CARE for AIDS. Thank you to Jay and Diane Strack, founders of Student Leadership University. Your belief and investment in my life as a teenager paved the way for me to lead CARE for AIDS well at such a young age. Thanks to the host of other mentors who poured into my life over the past thirty years, including Vince Cobb, Bryan Bartley, Joe Thomas, Peter Greer, and James Allison.

Unfortunately, this list is incomplete because so many people have shaped my life over the past three decades. This journey has been a testament to God's amazing grace and the strength of a community coming together for a common purpose. Thank you!

## CORNEL'S ACKNOWLEDGMENTS

I would like to take this opportunity to acknowledge the men and women who have played critical roles in my growth, becoming key reference points in my life. First, I would like to acknowledge my wife, Irene Onyango, who betted on me and agreed to walk this interesting journey by my side twelve years ago. Nyamalo, I am forever grateful. Second is my mother, Norah Atieno, who has been a pillar of strength and a rock in my life. For all her resilience and sacrifice to raise me into the man I have become, Mama asante sana.

I would also like to thank Samson Ojienda who baptized me and also introduced me to IMPACT Team and encouraged me to join. That is where it all began. I can't forget to mention Cindy Wilson, the founder of IMPACT, who took a chance on me and gave me the opportunity to become part of the IMPACT program and later recalled me to become the group leader of the class of 2002. I would also want to acknowledge Melanie Wilson who was the first group leader of the pioneer IMPACT Team and also paid part of my tuition fees at the seminary. My friend and colleague Steve Okoth is a pillar in our ministry. He has seen it all, right from the time CARE for AIDS (CFA) was just a concept. He came on board as the first employee to offer his accounting expertise at no cost. My heart also goes to all CFA employees in Nairobi, Kisumu, Mombasa, Dar es Salaam, Homabay, Kilifi, Mwanza, and America. Thank you for investing in CFA.

Lastly, I would not forget to acknowledge my five lovely children, Brian, Justin, Sherry, Collins, and Cornel, Jr. They have been sources of inspiration to me. Just because I would not like them to be raised up by any other person or entity, I want other children to experience the same by helping other parents to live a life beyond AIDS.

## TEAM ACKNOWLEDGMENTS

There are two people who worked so closely on this project that they are practically co-authors, but they don't desire any recognition and only wanted to help tell this story in the best way possible. We are forever indebted to Molly Heacock and Krista Morgan for helping bring this book to life and making us sound so good.

To the entire CARE for AIDS team, past and present, US and African, each of your stories may never be told in a book, but they deserve to be. You are amazing men and women who inspire us every day! CARE for AIDS has only reached this level of impact because of your daily dedication to sacrificially loving and serving the most vulnerable people whom others have over-looked.

Thank you to all US CARE for AIDS board members and our four chairmen over the last decade who led the board with great passion and wisdom: Mark Miller, Michael Ray, Cliff Robinson, and Randy Gravitt. Similarly, we want to thank the men and women of the Kenyan board who provide leadership on the ground. We want to honor the seven people who have served on the Kenyan board: Samuel Mwaniki, Olivia Achieng, Bernard Odoyo, Wallace Thaiya, Betty Githinji, Hannah Michuki, and Job Odour.

We are eternally grateful for every donor, big and small, who has believed enough in CARE for AIDS to invest your resources in our work.

Finally, thank you to every person who had a hand in making this book a reality: Brent Cole, Oust, Greenleaf Publishing, and Bobby Neptune.